Foreword

This year, the Young Writers' *Away With Words* competition proudly presents a showcase of the best poetic talent selected from thousands of up-and-coming writers nationwide.

Young Writers was established in 1991 to promote the reading and writing of poetry within schools and to the young of today. Our books nurture and inspire confidence in the ability of young writers and provide a snapshot of poems written in schools and at home by budding poets of the future.

The thought, effort, imagination and hard work put into each poem impressed us all and the task of selecting poems was a difficult but nevertheless enjoyable experience.

We hope you are as pleased as we are with the final selection and that you and your family continue to be entertained with *Away With Words Scottish, Irish & Welsh Verses* for many years to come.

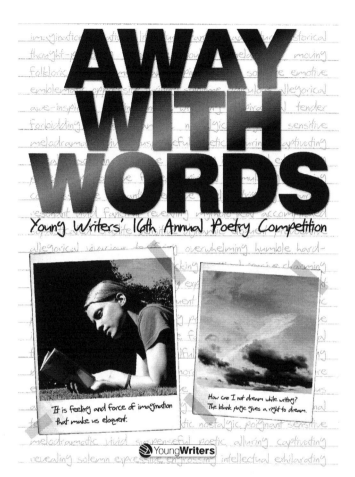

AWAY WITH WORDS

Young Writers' 16th Annual Poetry Competition

It is feeling and force of imagination that make us eloquent.

How can I not dream while writing? The blank page gives a right to dream.

YoungWriters

Scottish, Irish & Welsh Verses
Edited by Claire Tupholme

 Young**Writers**

First published in Great Britain in 2007 by:
Young Writers
Remus House
Coltsfoot Drive
Peterborough
PE2 9JX
Telephone: 01733 890066
Website: www.youngwriters.co.uk

SB ISBN 978-1 84602 919 6

Contents

Cameron Woodger (13)   55
Calum Stephen (13)   56
Craig Blackburn (13)   57
Chris Bailey   58
Alex Awramenko (13)   59
Kieran Ferguson (14)   60
Alice Allsop (13)   61
Rachel Midgley (13)   62
Amber Foreman (13)   63
Sean Tait (13)   64
Kirstin Leslie (13)   65

McLaren High School, Callander

Jamie Carr (12)   65
Laura MacDougall (12)   66
Henrietta Bowie (12)   67
Kirsten Innes (11)   68
Emma Buchanan (12)   69
Morag O'Shaughnessy (12)   70
Joshua McInnes (14)   70
Rachel Speirs (12)   71
Sam Wallace (12)   71
Mathew Simpson (12)   72
Corin Lang (12)   72
Hannah Petrie (12)   73
Ross Thompson (11)   73
Nikki Fisher (12)   74
Niamh Lee (11)   75
Tobias Shaw Paul (15)   76
James Gardner (12)   77
Adam Innes (13)   78
Liam Garvie (12)   79
Luke Melia (13)   80
Lucy Brooks (13)   80
David McDonald (13)   81
Scott Anderson (13)   81
David MacEachern (14)   82
Craig Campbell (13)   82
Mark Devlin (12)   83
Maureen Kimuyu (13)   83
Robbie Oman (13)   84

Andrew Orr (13)	85
Brooklyn Bell (12)	86
William Vernon (13)	87
Kaleidh Bruce (13)	88
Christopher Addison (13)	89
Amie Duffy (13)	90
James McBeath (13)	91

Nendrum College, Comber

James O'Lone (14)	91
Charlotte Walker (11)	92
Codie Nisbet (12)	92
Aaron English (14)	93
Ruth Barr (14)	93
Cassie Gilliland (11)	94
Rebecca Woods (14)	95
Kendal Jowett (13)	96
Ryan Craig (14)	96
Chloe Brown (11)	97
Thom Hinds (14)	97
Emma McManus (13)	98
Stephen Reid (14)	98
Martin Ferguson (13)	99
Emma Crawford (14)	99
Hannah Elizabeth Cash (11)	100
Connor Lynn (12)	100
Jason Cromie (12)	101
Jordan Spencer (11)	101
Aimee Orr (14)	102
Samantha Craigan (11)	102
Megan Stevenson (12)	103
Justyna Panas (12)	103
Ashleigh McQueen (12)	104
Laura McMillan (12)	104
Andrew McClure (11)	105
Danielle Toman (12)	105
Benjamin English (11)	106
Travis Heaybourne (12)	107
Rebecca Gibson (12)	107
Toni-Lee Martin (12)	108

St Christopher's School, Wrexham

Ysgol Bryn Elian, Colwyn Bay

The Poems

The Door

I stop
At the end of the drive,
Taking a breath,
Preparing myself,
The big white door,
Sits in darkness,
Like a negative
Of a black hole.

Scary,
Unwanted memories,
Hang around in the blurred shadows,
Beside a dim, welcoming light:
The relief
From the world,
But going to war.

Murmurs of voices,
And flashes of lights,
The fear is rising,
Tempted to see what
Awaits me within,
Clear, glass faces,
Staring back.

Shaking its hand,
In an old-fashioned way.
A tidal wave
Of heat flows out
Sucking me in, unable to go back,
Unwilling and afraid.

Walking in on the warzone,
Blocking it all out,
Escaping from the shouting,
To a world I want to be,
Then coming back to reality
To this world of misery.

Emma Merriman (14)
Currie Community High School, Currie

The Door

As I walk towards the door,
The bustle of people
Outside,
It is welcoming,
Overflowing bins,
That haven't been emptied for years,
Trees hang over the door,
It feels like summer's early.
The grey border of the door,
With glass inside,
A sterilised, clean look,
Yet this door is unusually
Welcoming.

As I move towards the door,
People stand
Behind like statues.
The glass has handprints
All over like people
Watching.
Metal handle with chips
That have been
There for a lifetime

As the door moves
Silently closer,
The trees tower over
Like friendly monsters.
A welcoming heat
Reminds me of before.
People chat,
Happily around me.
I get closer.

The white transfer
Now reads 'ush'
I 'ush'
The old chipped handle
Hard
The border of the door
Is dark and dirty,
The warmth
Inside and out
Shows summer's early.

Eilidh Nolan (14)
Currie Community High School, Edinburgh

The Door

The big golden gate
standing at the top
of the dark staircase.
Hints of the sun
bursting through the window,
contrasting with a shadow on the door.

Step by step
I walk up the golden path.
As I get closer
the door becomes more familiar
and as it glares at me
I recognise
the swirls on the wood.

The cold, smooth metal handle
gives off a familiar relaxing feel,
waiting to spring open.
I push down the handle;
the door brushes
along the sea-blue carpet
and I burst into a space
filled with memories.

Teri Webster (14)
Currie Community High School, Currie

The Blank Door

In my safe room of happiness
I discovered,
I had the black spot!
The darkness in my hand scared me.
The intensity made me dizzy,
As I left my sweet room
Behind me!

As I travelled down the hall
I took a right with a sudden jerk
Stopped to face the blank face of boredom,
Like eating cornflakes with no milk.
The eyes like they were frozen,
It had a fierce stare,
Like a great statue broken and accusing

As I edged closer to it, I could tell
It was gasping for air
As the hidden creature behind, beholds a smell:
Like dead maggots
This made everything grey
I slouched to peek through the side
But it slammed shut

The door was scarred
From previous slamming
Shadows crept beneath it.
I couldn't stop myself:
Now!
I placed my hand on the handle;
It was too late to turn away!

The coldness of the dusty gold handle
Gave me shivers!
No one ever touches it
And I wished I hadn't.
It creaked, I crept
As the handle pushed down
I blocked my nose
And the cracks where the door joined grinned.

Evaporating by boredom,
I craved not to go further as
I was choking on the fumes of
Strong aftershave and sweat.
I turned to the gravely yet annoying creature
It simply smiled: I sighed
Put down the sock,
I returned to my own washing.

Laura Waterson (14)
Currie Community High School, Currie

The Door

I'm standing at a distance
I notice:
Its mouth is missing,
Blank eyes stare blankly.
A blurred patterned face
Looks back at me
Excitement yet I get closer
Yet I get.

Edging closer,
Here I go
Closer, closer
Here I go
Anticipation bites my brain
Golden sun, golden handle
Glinting here, glinting there.

Anticipation building up
The backing white
Disappears.
Closer yet I get
Closer yet.

Reaching out I stop.
My anticipation suddenly drops
Time starts: I want to go in
Second time lucky . . .

Michael Murray (14)
Currie Community High School, Currie

What's Inside?

It's a door,
Not my door.
It's a door covered in
Stickers and posters.
It's not clearly visible
From where I stand.
It has a warm wooden
Look to it.
But cold shivers run
Through me.

The closer I get, I see
Colourful posters warning me,
Dare I enter?
Voices flowing through the door.
Like a baby bird
Learning to soar.

I hear noise, is it . . .
Wrappers?
Paper?
Laughs?
Cheers . . .
A clear gold mist
Shines through the window
In a cold hallway
The sun warms my cheek

A rough yet smooth
Texture on the door
Pulling me forward.
I stand at the open door
And I feel . . .
No hate
No joy
My plain emotion.

Behind it's his cold, messy arena.
With a small golden glow
Shining through the window.

It's his door
And his room.

Katherine Gibson (14)
Currie Community High School, Currie

The Door

The corridor seems long,
Longer than I thought,
The door is small,
I can see windows
Reflecting me from them,
My face surrounded by grey wood;
I begin walking.

The window revealing voices,
Light shining through,
My face becomes mosaic,
As I get closer to the door.

I stop at the towering door,
Smooth to the touch,
Light reflecting on the mirrored handle,
Revealing its past to me.

As I put my hand to the door:
What's behind?
Feeling so small,
As I push on the worn handle.

A wave of hot air hits my face,
I stop.
I stare around me:
So quiet and still,
I feel so alone,
As the door clicks behind me.

Natalie Faulds (14)
Currie Community High School, Currie

The Door

I can see my door.
Standing there;
Relying on its frame
For support.
The polished golden handle
Reflecting the light.
Anxious for me
To push it open!

I edge forward,
Everything now in focus:
The chipped paint
Around the edges
Like holes in a cardigan,
Leaving the yellow
Under the brown;
Bare.

Again I move forward.
My nose almost touching the door.
Frail and shaking,
It's rocking backwards
And forwards;
The windows open.

I start to move
My hand towards the handle.
As I hold the handle in my hand,
I think about its smooth feel,
Its soft touch, as soft
As an elderly handshake,
Its golden shine
And its warm touch.
I turn the handle.

I gently push open the big, heavy door.
Happiness rushes through my veins.
The door creaks me a 'hello'
As the cold welcoming air
Greets me while rushing through me.
I look around
At all of my possessions
And think, *I'm back.*

Mohammad Wasi Sheikh (14)
Currie Community High School, Currie

The Door

At first sight all you can think is 'bright'.
Bright grass-green large door
Standing in front of you.
Brass numbers and letter box
Reflecting the sun
In your face.
The closer you get
The more you notice
The roughness and the chips on the door.
Strong wooden door
Standing up
In the bad weather.
Not many scars even with the amount of pain it puts up with.
Stiff heavy door, nothing more.

Lucy Sutherland (14)
Currie Community High School, Currie

The Door

I got out of my car
Facing the door,
Looking at it,
Examining it,
Watching the movement of shadows
Through the opaque windows.

Walking towards the barrier of my house,
The smell of the bittersweet of my tea was growing,
Shadow of my dad,
Getting ready for work.
Sound of the TV blaring . . .

Football's on, Hearts beating Hibs 4-0,
Dad walking through,
Cursing at the TV
Hearts just scored,
Now it's 5-0.

Right up at the door,
Face to face,
As if we were about to fight,
The door swung open,
The smell of my tea was getting better, clearer
The door was bright and almost luminous
As if it was made for the king.

As I walked over the threshold,
All I could hear was my mum screaming with joy,
And Dad cursing on his way to work.

In the door in my nice warm home
Eating my sweet and sour chicken,
It was lovely,
I loved it.

Andrew McMillan (14)
Currie Community High School, Currie

The Door

A dark gravel path
crunches beneath my feet.
The crisp winter's air
chills my breath
and sends brutal shivers
down my spine.
Roses sit patiently
in a bed of sparkling frost.
Each petal is coated
in a layer of icy lace.

My eyes are met by light.
It is warm and sympathetic.
Shining through a glass panel door,
it lures me closer.

The streets are in darkness,
they have no voice.
I move briskly.
To my right a grey banister
sits slouched slightly
to my favour, its roots
embedded in the path.

Now standing on the doorstep,
almost able to smell the warmth,
I ring the bell.
Waiting, I stare into space.
I admire the stars and their powerful beauty.
I feel safe and happy
as the moon smiles down on me.

The door is opened.
I eagerly clamber in.
I push the door forwards.
With a single slam
I have left behind
Winter's bitter-sweet embrace.

Maeve Shaw (14)
Currie Community High School, Currie

The Door

Grass-green with
A sea-blue rim,
Windows like portholes.
As we approach,
My heart beats faster;
Thumping and pounding.

Stomach churning,
Like a windmill turning.
Looking: curtains;
Thick, pencil grey dust on top.
Dull green handles with grey
Peeking through.

Looking through the oval glass,
The receptionist sits.
Waiting,
Waiting on patients to enter.
Blood rushes through me,
Thump,
Thump.

Heels down hard,
Digging deeper,
Deeper,
Down into the concrete.
Negative thoughts run through me,
The door just stares.

Its green cold lips
Feel unwelcoming.
Resisting to go in,
My heart beats faster.
Thump,
Thump.

Green mouth opens wide,
I'm stuck, sucked in.
Trapped.
No turning back.
Walking through,
Friendly voices chirping,
Like conversations
At my funeral.

Kerry Mackay (14)
Currie Community High School, Currie

The Door

Lying in a bed
Looking at the wide double doors
Grey, blank, they are coloured
Feeling frightened
Squinting eyes
To see double doors

Wheely bed squeaks below
Going through
Heart thumps
Like a small child
Stamping their double feet

Smell whiffs
Into my nose
Teardrops from eyes
Doors swing -
Two double doors

Light bursts into the room
Doors behind me
Mask on face
Eyes close.

Charis McNair (14)
Currie Community High School, Currie

Party

A party was behind it.
But who was there?
Path slithering up to it,
Steps every so often.
It looked huge:
Bigger than me.
Mouth to the house,
Scary with dirty whiteness,
Moonlight reflecting off glass panels,
Nervous excitement accumulating.

I shuffled a little closer.
Muffled voices
Coming from inside.
Like a monster,
Tummy growling.
Hazy glass panels,
Staring back at me,
Light shining through,
Laser eyes.
Would have been shiny plastic
In its day.
I stumble
Odd height steps.

I moved along the path,
Muffled voices from inside,
Stumbling over occasional steps,
House towering down over me,
Intimidating fat features.
Glass eyes with white eyeliner
Watching.
Anticipation growing.

I lunged a little closer,
Loud laughter.
Teens talking.
Smell of Chinese takeout.
Last chance to turn and run.

Emma Forrest (14)
Currie Community High School, Currie

The Door

The cold breeze.
Pushing me on, from behind
The sun's glare.
Piercing my eyes
The shadows,
Moving behind the green glass,
Like fish in a pond.

Swinging in the wind.
Quadruplets,
Two sets of twins
Four doors.
Lots of noise, babbling
Movement!
Like sharks on the ocean floor.
People! Hundreds
Like the crowd at a football game.
Noise!
Like sports fans chanting.

My breath condensing,
Like a rain shower
Washing the glass.
Eyes, noses, looking my way
Wondering?
Wondering?
What will I do?

Cold, sticky - freezing skin
Silver, scratched, stained
Battered,
As if with a crowbar,
Heavier.
Heavier than my conscience
Breeze of fear, scary.

Noise -
A buzzing in my ear.
Eyes, staring!

Paul McFadden (14)
Currie Community High School, Currie

The Door

Waking up with the
Agonising pain of toothache,
The dreaded fear begun.
Strolling down the street,
Nearly there,
Soon I'll be in that dreaded chair.
Climbing up the dull black stairs,
Scared to death,
As I approach the grey
Dentist's chair.

Just like I remember it:
A white doorbell on the left,
Names on the right,
A round, shiny handle,
And mouth-like letter box,
A horrible reminder
Of what is lurking behind.

The terrifying sound
Of drills from the inside
Makes me freeze with fear,
Quivering like a jelly
I reach out to the bell
Thinking stupidly
It's only a door.

Standing forever
For the door to open,
No turning back now,
Noises becoming louder,
Me becoming more nervous;
Grabbing the cold brass handle
I push the heavy door
With a creaking sound.
Slowly stepping inside.

Ashleigh Dobie (14)
Currie Community High School, Currie

The Door

Stare back,
The door showing
Off, shiny gold handle
Asking for
A handshake. Staring me out,
Glowing glass, see the door.
Dark around.

I step, notice cracked
Glass,
Chipped wood.
Handle, rusty marks.
Don't want to shake his hand.
Skin, rough sandpaper.

Freezing feet. Still
Staring me out.
Reaching
For the handle.

Finally I get
To the handshake.
Coldest hand, wrinkly
Skin peeling
Already. I
Shake.

Freezing with every step.
Door behind me.
I pick up the paper
And go back to
The heat of the
Safehouse.

Patrick Hornig (14)
Currie Community High School, Currie

The Door

I look; the razor white,
like fearsome teeth,
I pause,
the door stares -
as I look I feel relief.
Tall, elegant, it's divine,
the letter box tapping, talking to me.
It's my friend,
gold handle beaming so bright
I smile in delight

As I approach I hear rain,
drip, drip, drip.
I want to go, be free.
The patterned windows filled with glee;
they are dancing in the rain.

Handle so smooth,
like curves,
welcoming to touch.
Silence,
apart from rain.
The razor white,
a little warm.
The warrior stands so tall,
keeps all out,
I feel a breeze,
I start to shake;
want to go.

As I open the guard,
it squeaks with rage.
Darkness all around,
car headlights like peering eyes,
watching every move.
I look back. My friend looks sad,
'Why have you left me?' he says.

Paul McGovern (14)
Currie Community High School, Currie

The Scary Door

As I leave my house,
I start walking.
As I look up on it,
The dark green paint,
Taunts me by reflecting
The sun in my eyes.

I get closer
I hear laughing,
Trying to mock me.
As I think about
The cramped space behind it.
Sadness has befallen me.

As I get closer still
The window seems to grow.
As I look through
I see the faint outline
Of my little brother laughing,
Laughing at me.

I near the door
And reach out for the handle.
But as I pull the handle
It grabs me,
With a cold metallic touch.

I squeeze into the small
Cramped space
And get ready
For the long journey ahead.

Jack Yourston (14)
Currie Community High School, Currie

My Favourite Door

Standing looking at the door
The heat sneaking from the gap along the floor
From the floor to the ceiling
The bright brown door looks appealing
Its rectangle shape like a chocolate bar
The door is standing ajar
I want to go through
So I can do
My own things!

As I step closer
More pleased - day's over
I hear the computer silently mumbling
The door blowing
Back and forward
Back and forward
As it blows a bit of light shows
Like it is waving me in:
Inviting.

As I take a step nearer -
It becomes clearer
The mumbling sound.
The handle round.
Perfume streams up my nose
Can't wait till my trouble goes
Can't wait till I'm in there -
With no other care:
Just me.

I take a few steps more
I touch the door:
The metal is warm
I push to get out of the storm
A mess, the way I like it.
But my mum still has a fit
But I don't care -
It's *mine.*

Now I'm on my own
It feels more like home,
Just my stuff.
No more people in a huff.
My lilac room with just me
Where I want to be
On my own
In peace.

Nicole Cunningham (14)
Currie Community High School, Currie

The Classroom Door

As I approached the dull, dusty red door
I stopped
I thought about what might be store for me
through the red door
I continued
until I got to the door
I stopped
and looked through the window
at the horrid glare of the books
paper and pencils.

The atmosphere inside was murky, cold and dull
like a bottomless pit of silence
As I looked down
I saw an old mouldy carpet
with mud stains and gum
stuck to the dusty floor.

I started to open the door
and quickly remembered
I was not alone!

Benji Hardie (14)
Currie Community High School, Currie

My Worst Nightmare

My worst nightmare
chipping away at my confidence
dull, glaring, laughing
the distant door,
eye set upon
the golden handle.

Closer, closer,
bad thoughts
whirling around in my mind,
blue-ish blackened giant
full of surprises
like opening presents,
what is lurking
behind the dental door?

Taking deep breaths
my slackened hand -
the blinding handle,
where in contact.
The noise of the
worn out handle
screeching while turned,
like someone screaming
I step into
the blackened hole!

Narrow, dull hall
pictures staring me out
noisy dental equipment,
like spoilt children whining,
I felt ill, intimidated,
I sit
until I hear,
'Nicole Kennedy'
My head sinks into my top!

Nicole Kennedy (14)
Currie Community High School, Currie

New York

I stood there,
Waiting on my luggage,
Looking round to the exit,
Catching glimpses of the wonderful world,
I was about to enter.
Huge buildings
Catching my attention.

Making my way through
The crowd.
Can't hear taxis no more;
It is too loud.
Shouts, cheers, laughs
The noise of travel.

Nerves tingling throughout
My body,
As if I were about
To take a winning penalty.
Suitcases in and out my feet
Edging closer to the door.

My hand finally reaches the door.
Cold as ice
The smooth relaxed sound
Of the door opening
Felt so nice.
For miles only seeing cars,
Water, buildings,
New York neck.

Michael Melville (14)
Currie Community High School, Currie

The Door

The door searches me,
Fresh chocolate orange door,
Its shape is an oblong.
The house windows appear open,
Welcoming me.

A plastic gold handle,
Alone;
Markings from times gone by,
As flat as a pancake
No ridges or bumps,
The stiff metal letterbox
Hard and proud.

One eye is hidden,
One ready to be opened.
Sound inside obstructed
By the heavy door,
Thick brown walls on either side
Like bars of chocolate.

I see through the frame
A dark red, velvet carpet
Like a river of blood.
It is waiting for footsteps.

I step closer as a gust of wind
Makes me shiver -
Is this a signal
Of things to come?
I turn the key;
It clicks,
The handle
Warm and welcoming.
I push down,
People inside
Alerted by the noise.

Deep breath.
The last time wasn't good;
A horrible smell of food
Attacks my nostrils;
I'm seen as an intruder -
A different age from them,
My body surrounded
By the grey and old.

Scott Thomson (14)
Currie Community High School, Currie

Jamie

My cousin Jamie likes playing Fireman Sam
He's been to every fire in town.
My grandad is Fireman Steele
He helps put out the fires.

My cousin Jamie likes playing farms
He looks after his cows, Jessie and Bessie,
Making sure they are OK
And have food to eat.

My cousin Jamie likes playing boats
He drives the boats and radios in
To say he's coming into the harbour,
He fights off the pirates.

So that's my three-year-old cousin
After playing with his grandad
He goes away home
And it's a quiet house again.

Laura James (12)
Deans Community High School, Livingston

Whispers In The Graveyard

(Inspired by the novel)

Mum and Dad are married
And life's a living hell
They shout and argue all the time
I've no one I can tell
They've decided to live apart
And I've been given a choice
Mum sounds sad and
So does Dad's voice
I decided to stay with Dad
But through time I think it's bad
I feel so sad.
My dad's an alcoholic
He drinks all the time
No wonder my mum left
She knows my dad's a swine.
He drinks all the money
There's no food for me to eat
Sometimes he can hardly stand
On his own two feet.
I hate the thought of school
I go there every day
I am bullied and I am picked on
And have no friends who will play.
Mr Watking is so nasty
He's a teacher at the school
I dread the thought of seeing him
Because he makes me feel a fool
No matter what I do
Or how hard that I might try
He always finds a fault
And he makes me want to cry.
I suffer from dyslexia
And no one really knows
If someone were to find out
They would tell everyone they know.

I am bullied at the moment
And no one really cares
That's why I visit the graveyard
Because I am so scared.
I find it really calming,
I find it so rare,
Because I can talk and share my thoughts
And feel there are voices there.
They're digging up the graveyard
There are bodies everywhere
There's a disease in the ground
And no one knows it's there
This is my secret place, no one knows I am here
They wouldn't think of looking
It's a place of dug up ground.

Jamie Green (12)
Deans Community High School, Livingston

Art

Art is my subject, you can cut and play
and even make models out of hardened clay.

The picture I made was gold and blue
and I created a shine with PVA glue.

It's very much fun and not even hard
the design I made I used felt and card.

Art is fun and easy to do
and you can cut out things and colour in too.

Josh Fortune (12)
Deans Community High School, Livingston

Books

Books are a maze that is far from over
You can be at the end but be at the beginning
They come on their own as twins or as triplets
They all have names like me or you
They all look different and have something to say true or not.

Robbie Baird (12)
Deans Community High School, Livingston

Rugby

Balls are flying, everyone's diving.
People are spearing, everyone cheering.
Kicking the ball, the players jump tall.
Scoring a try, everyone's high.

Gary McGurk (12)
Deans Community High School, Livingston

In Geography Class

In geography class you learn about climate
the teacher says, 'Homework,'
and they all whine about it.
The sun is out, it shines in our eyes
everybody wishes it was lunchtime
so they can eat a few pies.
The teacher talks about temperature
what a lot of pressure
some people are chatting,
'Listen! I don't want to hear another peep!'
although half the class are fast asleep.

Leanne Paterson (13)
Farr High School, Thurso

What Is The Moon?

The moon is a white bobble,
Floating over a black Christmas tree.

It is a marshmallow,
On a black cup of coffee.

It is a mouldy bit of cheese,
Sitting in a dark cupboard.

It is a white oval rubber,
Lying on a black table.

It is a cup of milk,
Warming up on a black stove.

It is a silver plate,
On a black tablecloth.

It is a white pupil,
Lying in a black eye.

The moon is a light bulb,
In a black room.

Lucinda Dawson (12)
Farr High School, Thurso

Happiness

Happiness is yellow and orange.
It smells like blooming flowers.
Happiness tastes like chocolate.
Happiness sounds like your favourite song.
It feels like candyfloss.
Happiness is yellow and orange.

Claire Reid (12)
Farr High School, Thurso

Slow Dance

Have you ever watched kids,
On a merry-go-round?
Or listened to the rain,
Slapping on the ground?
Ever followed a butterfly's erratic path
Or gazed at the sun into the fading night?

You better slow down,
Don't dance so fast,
Time is short,
The music won't last.

Do you run through your day,
On the fly?
When you ask 'how are you?'
Do you hear a response?
When the day is done,
Do you lie in your bed
With the next hundred chores
Running through your head?

You better slow down,
Don't dance so fast.
Time is short,
The music won't last.

Ever told your child,
'We'll do it tomorrow?'
And in your haste
Not see his sorrow?
Ever lost touch,
Let a good friendship die
Because you never had the time,
To call and say hi?

You better slow down,
Don't dance so fast.
Time is short,
The music won't last.

When you run to get somewhere,
You miss half the fun in getting there.
When you worry and hurry through the day,
It is like an unopened gift,
Thrown away.

Life is not a race,
Do take it slower.
Hear the music,
Before the song is over.

Jessica Sandison (14)
Farr High School, Thurso

The Wave

The wave was coming closer
It was like a great big roller coaster,
This was the greatest one
It glimmered in the morning sun,
As it came nearer,
I saw it a bit clearer.

I started to paddle,
Making sure I was stable
The wave caught me and sucked me in,
I stood up with a great big grin
I was riding the wave,
The biggest that the sea gave.

I looked around as it tumbled forwards,
Riding the wave that was pushing me shorewards
It was the best thing ever,
Nothing could ever be better.

Caitlin Macleod (13)
Farr High School, Thurso

The Soldiers' Dare

The war goes on and on,
It's all just a great big con.
Your best friend being a long and powerful arm,
Which could do your enemy a lot of harm.
Trusting a rifle to save your life.
It's do or die out there,
That's the soldiers' dare.

Hitting onto a beach with very little cover,
Not aware that you could be killed there and then.
Digging trenches for safety,
A place to keep you warm, secure and sheltered.
Trying not to think of civilisation,
Or the warmness of home.
You just want to make it out alive,
To see your loved one.
It's do or die out there,
That's the soldiers' dare.

Bombs flying over your head,
Mortar flying, just missing your body.
Seeing a good friend getting buried,
Or even putting bits of him in a bag from a raid.
Facing the limits,
Being the miracle.
Receiving letters, what a feeling,
For those who don't, what a heartbreaker.
You only want to hear from your relatives,
It might be your last.
It's do or die out there,
That's the soldiers' dare.

Andrew Henderson (14)
Farr High School, Thurso

The Evil Snowman

Christmas had passed,
Not long did it last.

Outside was so chilly,
So cold you'd turn silly.

Outside was pure white,
No snowman in sight.

Their presents were gone,
So they searched until dawn.

Only to find nothing,
The kids were not laughing.

But over last night,
The snowman grew sight.

He started to walk,
Then he started to talk.

This evil white snowman,
Will do whatever he can.

To take all your toys,
And all children's joys.

Morgan Russell (13)
Farr High School, Thurso

Depression

Depression is grey and the darkest black.
It smells of venison and burning plastic.
Depression tastes of sorbet and crème fraise.
Depression sounds like nails scraping down glass.
It feels like a cold bed on a winter's night.
Depression is grey and the darkest black.

Tara Mackay (12)
Farr High School, Thurso

What Is The Moon?

The moon is a big round cheese,
Lying on black burnt toast.

It is a pale yellow balloon,
Floating in the winter nights.

It is a yellow tennis ball,
Swimming in the dark blue sea.

It is a white volleyball,
Kicked high in the blue sky.

It is a white dot,
Pricked on black paper.

It is a small piece of chewing gum,
Sticking on a black road.

It is the lamp between the trees,
Lighting up the nights.

Clara Doehl (12)
Farr High School, Thurso

What Is The Moon?

The moon is a white pan drop
floating in space

It is a disco ball
turning in darkness

It is a smiley face
on a black picture background

It is a pile of squirty cream
on a black kitchen worktop

It is a bowl of ice cream
on a jet-black carpet.

Emma Macleod (12)
Farr High School, Thurso

A Friendship Recipe

A friend is like my favourite meal
A bunch of salad with apple peel
Make a biscuit in a bowl
And make it heart-shaped
To show their soul
And for dessert
Some apple pie
And add a dove
So they wouldn't lie
Serve it up for you
And your friend
And once you eat it
Your friendship won't end.

Maria Cesa (14)
Glenburn School, Greenock

The War Memorial

Standing proud,
Representing Air Cadets,
My uniform pressed and tidy,
My beret tight,
The day, cold and calm,
Looking at the memorial,
A lump grew in my throat,
Marching forward,
Halting and laying the wreath,
I saluted,
Thinking of the past,
People and ghosts watching me,
Standing proud.

Cameron Robb (13)
Lockerbie Academy, Lockerbie

Wee Lassie Fae Troon

There was a wee lassie,
A note she wrote doon.
This wee lassie,
She was fae Troon.

Up tae Glasgae,
Doon tae Troon.
I'm a wee lassie,
Noo I'll play a tune.

Gee us a stone,
Gee us some money.
I will complain,
Bees, gee us your honey.

Lassie, lassie up the street,
Lassie across the road.
Gee us a sweet,
Gee us a toad.

Lassie fae Troon,
Lassie fae Glasgae.
I will play a merry tune,
All the way.

Lassie stop blowing yer whistle,
I'll throw a thistle.

I'll make a type o' tartan,
Up the Nile.
I will cook haggis in a pan,
I'll paint ye a tile.

There was a wee lassie,
A note she wrote doon.
This wee lassie,
She was fae Troon.

Kerry-Louise Moore (12)
Lockerbie Academy, Lockerbie

Ma Cat Tam

Ma cat Tam
He once bit my ma
He came creeping up
Behind her
She didnae have a clue
He slithered o'er the carpet
The sofa and chair
I watched fae the doorway
'No, Tam don't you dare!'
He leapt three feet upwards
And forward all at once
My ma was watching telly
When he landed on her heed, then
Tam went for lunch
He totally misjudged things
He fell in his watter
Now Tam lives in the garden.

Ciaran Traquair (12)
Lockerbie Academy, Lockerbie

Chocolate

Chocolate after dinner,
is what I like the most.
I like it with my breakfast,
especially on my toast.
I'll eat it on the sofa,
I'll eat it on the floor
and when I've finished all of that
I'll beg and beg for more!

Sally-Anne Aitken (12)
Lockerbie Academy, Lockerbie

Diamonds Are Forever

Sparkling in the daytime light,
Or placed alone in the darkness of the night,
So expensive they can be,
But they are the only jewel for me.

Diamonds are forever,
They can be as light as a feather,
They can be used on many occasions
Or for an engagement celebration.

You can find them in a shop down the street
Or passed down generations to keep,
You can do whatever you want with them
As they are much better than a gem.

Diamonds are forever,
They can be as light as a feather,
They can be used on many occasions
Or for an engagement celebration.

Diamonds are forever!

Claire-Marie Warwick (12)
Lockerbie Academy, Lockerbie

A Flame

A flame can be a thing of beauty
It can flicker and dance in the breeze
It can bring joy in the form of a candle bringing light
A mixture of red, orange and yellow

It can be hypnotic

A flame can be a thing of destruction
A building can be devastated
A single flame from a match
A flame that spreads and swarms
Taking everything in its path

It can be hypnotic.

Adam Billson (13)
Lockerbie Academy, Lockerbie

Anger/Relaxation

Anger
Anger is the colour red.
Anger looks like red boiled sweets.
Anger sounds like a volcano ready to erupt.
Anger feels like you are about to scream.
Anger smells like loud, roaring fire.
Anger tastes like hot chicken curry.

Relaxation
Relaxation is the colour purple.
Relaxation looks like dolphins swimming in the distance.
Relaxation sounds like soothing music.
Relaxation feels like you are in a warm soapy bath.
Relaxation smells like scented candles.
Relaxation tastes like a glass of wine.

Elsa Leslie (12)
Lockerbie Academy, Lockerbie

The Newcomer

The girl came from England
No one accepted her
Especially the boy that sat next to her
The girl got bullied because of her skin
Her mum said
It doesn't matter what skin you're in
But the girl still was bullied when she went to school
Everyone just laughed at that boy being a fool
The girl went home bruised and hurt inside
She just wished everything would wash away with the tide.

Isla Shea (13)
Lockerbie Academy, Lockerbie

Change

The sun's power is weakened by the wind
The green is receding to the strength of reds and browns
Coal and flame keep out approaching cold
Stopping it at winter's gates.

Horns of howling wind
Roar as they meet reddened trees
Bite of cold and steaming breath
Remind that the warmth is gone.

The emergence of morning sun
Shines down revealing the beauty of it all
The colour of trees is the new light in this landscape
Autumn is upon the world.

Rory McKie (17)
Lockerbie Academy, Lockerbie

Closest Friend

Side by side.
We sit on top of the barn, on the cold stone slabs.
The frozen air wrapping around us like a thick blanket of ice
Yet we did not want to be in the warmth inside,
We wanted to be together - alone outside,
We didn't speak though.
There was nothing left to say.
We had spoken for hours that day
But even so,
There was nowhere else we would rather be
Than where we were right then.
Side by side.

Gwen Dupre (13)
Lockerbie Academy, Lockerbie

I Live For The Weekend

I live for the weekend
To step on the ice
To play my sport
Ice hockey.

I live for the weekend
For the puck to drop
For the game to begin
Ice hockey.

I live for the weekend
For the ice to spray
For punches to land
Ice hockey.

I live for the weekend
To score some goals
To hit some players
Ice hockey.

Murray McLachlan (13)
Lockerbie Academy, Lockerbie

Friends

Friends, friends, friends,
We all need friends,
Tall friends, short friends,
Shy friends, bold friends,
We all need friends.

Having friends is what makes us human,
Friends, they're our blue skies,
Friends are little butterflies.

Friends are always there for you,
Friends will see you cry,
Friends will always care for you,
And they will never pass you by.

Flin Allen-Henderson (13)
Lockerbie Academy, Lockerbie

Dreamers

A dreamer (single)

You dream in metaphors
and have done, since the age of innocence ended
with metamorphosis abandoning you
somewhere most other people don't go

the painful interior of your skull
echoes into your life, your motivation is all wrong
and you push yourself into corners intentionally
reading everything as judgement time

and the silver on your right hand
only serves to remind you that it is not on your left.

A dreamer (attached)

Too much, a heavy-handed tackle by fate
leads to everything on one plate by your bedside table
from three weeks ago

the red lines are all you see on the sheet
the mistakes, the pressure and the corrections
rolling over on the pillow to slam your face into a wall

yesterday is now a memory
of someone who calmed you in spite of your tornado
of language and abuse threatening to cut your throat in half
as the scathing words fell from a loosely wired thinking box

yesterday is the one who kept calling
and calling
and calling
(ring ring)
to see how things were upon cloud number 17
as you told yourself all was fine and you could handle it all

the someone who stopped the train tracks from disappearing
into a non-existent horizon of badly painted landscapes.

Jennifer Owen (16)
Lockerbie Academy, Lockerbie

The Queen's Party

Standing outside, waiting to go in
Jugglers and clowns fooling around
Chitty Chitty Bang Bang goes past
But we have passports out to be allowed in.

We're in at last, through the huge gate
Guards standing like statues
Everyone happy and cheery
Waiting to see what's behind the main door.

Out through the back
The hugest garden I've ever seen
Picnic hampers and cameras given out
The food so good it melted in my mouth.

Walking around, glimpsing famous authors
Jacqueline Wilson and J K Rowling are just two
Children crowding round to get autographs
I join the queue and wait my turn.

There she is
The woman I've been waiting to see
No hat this time but still a smile
I can't believe I've met the Queen.

An announcement says it's time to go and see
What's been promised the best bit of the day
We go and take our seats
To see what's going to happen in the play.

The Queen's handbag had been stolen
But the goodies found it in the end
I had a great day
I wished it wouldn't end.

Rebecca Donaldson (13)
Lockerbie Academy, Lockerbie

School On Fridays

Registration, get clocked in,
Teachers ask if everyone is there.
The tannoy is where I stare,
Bell rings,
I go to class,
Everyone is rushing very fast,
Period one and two PE,
Boo hoo hoo.

Five minutes 'til interval,
Soon people will be having snacks and drinks,
Mmmm, everybody thinks,
Period three, French,
Bonjour,
Period four, art,
I don't think we will be making a chart.

Lunch,
Yum, I think as I munch,
Telly goes off,
Period 5, English,
Pens and pencils at the ready,
I am starting to write my critical essay,
My writing may be a bit messy,
Bell goes,
At last, period six, maths,
I stare at the clock,
As it goes tick-tock,
Off goes the bell,
I go to the bus,
The driver makes a terrible fuss.

Victoria Morgan (14)
Lockerbie Academy, Lockerbie

My Muddled Life

I jumped up one morning,
and woke out of bed.
I drank my toast,
and then I was fed.
I ate my juice,
and gulped up the stairs.
I brushed on my clothes,
and shoved on my teeth.
I rode out of the doorway,
and walked onto my bike.
I collapsed into school,
and I ran on my seat.
I finished my school work,
and dumped school.
I popped on homewards,
and cycled into the door.
I fell to the kitchen,
and popped to the floor.
I walked into the stairs,
and up through my door.
I put on my prayers,
and said my night nights.
I switched off my bed
and jumped into the light,
all because you kissed me goodnight!

Shona Carmichael (13)
Lockerbie Academy, Lockerbie

Shoes

There are hundreds of shoes you can get,
All different colours, yellow, green and blue.
All sorts of makes, Converse or Lacoste,
Vans and K Swiss to name a few.

The prices vary, expensive and cheap,
It depends on the shop or even the place.
M & S, Priceless and New Look are some
Of the shops where you could make haste!

Styles - now there's a lot of them!
Trainers, espadrilles, flip-flops and pumps,
Baseball boots, sandals, Ugg boots galore,
All of these come up trumps!

Hundreds of designs that can be found,
Polkadots, stripes and checks have been made,
And different fabrics, leather or wood,
Cotton or plastic, furry or suede.

There are hundreds of shoes you can get,
Different colours, prices, styles in shops,
Disliked by some, bought by many,
But personally, I love my flip-flops!

Kathleen Kelly (13)
Lockerbie Academy, Lockerbie

Cats

Daytime cats are always sleeping or eating,
They are never playful or up and about,
But at night
They hunt and they run,
They bounce and pounce and sneak and creep,
Looking for mice to gobble up.
They don't and won't share with other cats,
They would rather fight for their food.
After they eat, they move stealthily
Into other cats' houses,
They prowl into the kitchens then peer for food,
They jump onto the kitchen table to get a better view,
The cat springs
And devours the meal in one.
The full feline runs out,
And back to its own humble abode.
Quickly creeping past the stairs
Where the enraged dog lies.
Jumping onto the window sill,
Sits on the pillow
And falls asleep.

Philippa Billson (13)
Lockerbie Academy, Lockerbie

Bumblebees

Bumblebees, yellow and black
Flying in the air
All hairy and fat
6 legs, 2 eyes and a nose
Getting pollen out a rose.

They fly up high
They swoop down by
Round and round
They make a sound
In and out, out and in
Buzz buzz, that's their thing.

But if danger comes their way
There is only one safe way
A secret weapon that they've got
To protect them against harmful things
It's the dreaded sting.

They put their bums up in the air.
Hoping that God will answer their prayers
It's over now, but oh, what's wrong
This is no fake, lying, not awake
They are dead for goodness sake.

Rhiana Maxwell (13)
Lockerbie Academy, Lockerbie

My Bub

My grandad's name was Ron,
I had him till I was twelve,
It wasn't really very long.

He was quite small,
He had white hair,
The funny thing was
There wasn't a lot of it there.

He had yellow fingers,
And liked to smoke,
But really, he was a nice bloke.

He made the best
Egg, chips and beans,
He wore a string vest,
And he was definitely not mean.

He'd give us 10p,
To go get some sweets,
But then he'd expect change!

I miss my Bub.

Ferne Lambert-Gorwyn (13)
Lockerbie Academy, Lockerbie

My Weird Day

I woke up in the morning and jumped right out of bed,
I opened up the curtains and everything was red.
I went downstairs to tell my mum and dad
I opened up the door and everything was mad.
My brother was hanging from the light
My sister and dad were having a fight.
My dog was sitting in a pot
My mum was laughing quite a lot.
I had my breakfast, steak and chips
Then left for school, licking my lips.
I crossed the road with a fireman
The lollipop lady drove by in his van.
I skipped along the bright red road
There were rabbits and monkeys and even a toad.
Children were dressed with tights on their head
And were acting as if they had never been fed.
They were on their hands and knees eating mud and grass
The whole school had gone crazy and it wasn't just my class.
The day was weird and wonderful but went by fast
It's time for bed, I've had great fun, I hope that it will last!

Nicole Lawrie (13)
Lockerbie Academy, Lockerbie

My Fears

There are only three things that scare me,
These things terrify me the most.
They're not anything unusual,
They're not bats or rats or a ghost.

Spiders are number one,
I don't like the way they move and crawl,
Whenever I see one,
It makes me shout and bawl.

Lifts are second on my list,
I don't like those big heavy doors
And the way they move,
Going higher and higher to each and every floor.

Heights are last but not least on my fears list,
I never used to be scared of heights,
But one day I fell from a high tree,
Ever since that day
Heights have scared me.

Ally Stewart (14)
Lockerbie Academy, Lockerbie

My School Day

Jump out of bed,
Open the curtains,
Fly down the stairs,
Turn on the shower,
Lovely and warm,
Then scrub-a-dub-dub,
Fly up the stairs,
Chuck my clothes on,
Nice and smart,
Down for breakfast,
Grab a bowl,
Whip out the cereal,
Pour fresh milk,
Do my hair,
Brush my hair,
I am all ready,
Mum starts the engine,
To the bus stop,
I wait and wait,
Rolling to the stop,
Jump on,
Grab a seat,
And here I am on my way,
Chat to friends and giggle,
The start of a school day.

Ewan Paul (14)
Lockerbie Academy, Lockerbie

The Sky Poem

The ocean above
Like a big, bright, bulging ball.

Changes its colour,
Like a chameleon,
Red or black or blue.

Clouds float,
Like sheep in an open field.

Rain and thunder sound,
Like marbles thrown on a floor.

Falling snow is soft,
Like a sponge.

The open globe gives us space,
To fly to other countries,
To freedom.

Steven Gray (13)
Lockerbie Academy, Lockerbie

My Pony

I remember when I got her,
The sunshine in the sky,
The beautiful pony standing proud,
The sparkle in her eyes,

I let her in the field,
So she could run about,
She was so happy,
I could see that without a doubt,

She cantered and galloped,
Around and around,
My first ever pony
She made me so proud.

Laura Wilson (14)
Mackie Academy, Stonehaven

Dolphin Day

I was filled with fear
As a torpedo-like animal
Was flying towards me

With its great big fin
And its great big tail
I honestly thought it was as big as a whale

They told us to swim out
Gave the creatures a shout
Then they jumped right out

It gave me the fright of my life
The fear in my chest was like the stab of a knife
That's what they do in everyday life

In all it was a very good day
I would have to say
I really did enjoy watching the dolphins play.

Jamie Davidson (13)
Mackie Academy, Stonehaven

Horse Riding

The feeling was amazing, I felt so proud,
I was moving so quickly it seemed so loud,
We whizzed past roads, bushes and trees,
I was so happy and full of glee.

The pony was fat, though gentle and sweet,
Despite her size, she had very clumsy feet,
Her tail was swishing, her eyes so bright,
She was such a beautiful sight.

She was hot and tired, and became very smelly,
Her knees looked as if they had turned to jelly,
We took her back, and washed her down,
And the next day, we took her back round.

Anna Cranston (13)
Mackie Academy, Stonehaven

That's Flow, My Cat

Flow is my cat
All fluffy and fat
She's ginger, white and black
That's Flow, my cat

Tuna is her favourite food
But if she likes it that depends on her mood
Her favourite toy is her fluffy white mouse
But then she takes it and runs into her house

One day she ran far away
And never came back till the very next day
I never knew I could miss her so much
It was like taking the quack out of a duck

When she came back she was as fat as a mat
And as hungry as a rat
But oh well that's Flow, my cat
All fluffy and fat!

Kimberley Preston (13)
Mackie Academy, Stonehaven

Wind Tunnel

I stepped through the door and was lifted into the air
It was as if I was a bird flying without a care
Then it was over and I came crashing to the ground
Maybe a bear pulled me down.

I was ready to go again
It was like a one way lane
Soon enough I was back up
The air was milk and I was a cat lapping it up.

Back on my feet I knew the ropes that held me there
Were billions of particles of air
I suppose even if you are small
In great numbers you can be tall.

Cameron Woodger (13)
Mackie Academy, Stonehaven

Sheikra - The Ultimate Roller Coaster

Queuing for what seems like an age
Trapped in a crowd like a bird in a cage
Gradually advancing up the stair
My impatience turning into despair.

Then as I reach the front of the queue
The massive steel monster comes into view
As I climb into the front of the car
I hear the clattering down of the safety bar.

As it starts to climb straight to the top
Fear grips me, I want it to stop
Hanging vertically at two hundred feet high
I'm terrified; feel I'm going to die.

As soon as it drops I'm hit by shock
At the thrill of falling, just like a rock
It reaches the bottom, goes into a loop
My insides seem to have turned to soup.

All too soon, it comes to an end
One more drop and then the final bend
Full of adrenaline I want it to last
I wish it hadn't finished so fast.

Some people compare a roller coaster to life
They say it's full of joy, trouble and strife
When I think about it, it can't be true
Because in life you can choose what to do.

Calum Stephen (13)
Mackie Academy, Stonehaven

Bird To America

There were large wings of an angel,
With an engine like a thousand lion roars,
The large body of the white bird.

My heart was pounding, as I stepped on the bird,
For it was the first time I flew with Bluebird,
I was excited and scared at the same time.

As the plane lifted off,
The engine like a thousand lion roars got faster and faster,
And with a bang the bird was off like the speed of light.

I saw the sky above the clouds,
It looked like white candyfloss,
But not the stuff you can eat.

But then the pilot said we're ready to land,
Just as I had begun to get over my fear,
And with a thump the white bird landed.

As I stepped off the plane,
The heat outside was as hot as a boiler,
The hottest I have ever felt.

When we arrived at the hotel,
There as a big sign that said,
Welcome To America.

Craig Blackburn (13)
Mackie Academy, Stonehaven

Roller Coaster

Waiting in the line half a mile long.
People screaming like monkeys in a cage.
Everyone quiet, quiet as a mouse but in their eyes only fear.

I wait in the line to the monster, the monster made of steel!
As it takes me up into the clouds,
I hear the creaks and cracks of the track!
As I hang over the drop my heart stops beating
And for that split second there is only silence
As the wind hits my face.

As I fall at lightning speed the screams and cries begin to change.
I wait for my scream to pelt out of my mouth
But instead comes the sound of excitement.

It is as if it isn't a monster but in fact an eagle
And I'm soaring above the clouds.

When the graceful bird comes to a halt
I look at the line half a mile long
And before I know it, it is once again my turn to fly.

Chris Bailey
Mackie Academy, Stonehaven

Viva La Bus Crash

My family went off to our holiday on the plane,
To an island that was a part of Spain,
And we took the bus instead of the train,
To a city which had no fame.

On the way back, the bus smelt like salt,
It drove over a rock, and came to a halt.
The bus driver was an idiot, so it was all his fault.
They were sending another bus, I was told.

As the bus sat still, we sat on a wall,
The tyre was burst like a deflated basketball,
Sitting was boring and very dull,
Now I wish I never taken that bus at all.

No one spoke our English language,
After all, everyone was Spanish,
When the bus came our troubles had vanished,
And after that, we learnt to speak Spanish.

Alex Awramenko (13)
Mackie Academy, Stonehaven

My First Day At School

The fear welled inside me,
My first day of school,
Got to be brave,
Got to stay cool.

The big kids in the hallways,
The stories I hear,
They fight like lions,
This defines fear.

These giants all push,
And they all shout,
Like the engine of a car,
I really want out.

And then the classes,
I can't subtract,
Science is impossible,
And that's a fact.

And then it was over,
Saved by the bell,
Safe 'til tomorrow,
Then back to the hell . . .

Kieran Ferguson (14)
Mackie Academy, Stonehaven

Wiggle Wiggle

Wiggle wiggle, just fall out
I felt I wanted to scream and shout
My first tooth was on its way
Hip hip hip hooray

I was as excited as a bee
I was going to get my 50p
I would write a letter just to ask
To keep my tooth to make the memory last

When it finally came out
I jumped and screamed and ran about
I ran downstairs to tell my dad
Nothing could possibly make me sad

I sat and thought what to write
This was going to be a very long night
I wanted to keep my tooth just for me
The fairy couldn't use it as a piano key

That night I went to sleep
Promising I wouldn't peep
I woke the next day to find
My 50p and my tooth sitting behind.

Alice Allsop (13)
Mackie Academy, Stonehaven

My First Teacher

It may have been the scariest experience I'd ever had.
The way she stared at me, her face was so mad.
My friend and I were just painting away
Then we decided to put it everywhere, she didn't know what to say.

She just stood there in silence and looked everywhere.
She started to scream and shout, we thought she wouldn't care.
Our faces were pale and we had tears in our eyes.
We tried to blame someone else but she knew they were lies.

We just stood there shaking then started to cry.
So she stopped all her shouting then gave a big sigh.
And then showed us that we had broken a rule.
That was my first teacher in primary school.

But I was so young I thought I'd forget it
But not this time, I remember every bit.
I avoided her as much as I could until the end of school
The one thing I remembered was never to break that rule.

Rachel Midgley (13)
Mackie Academy, Stonehaven

Casey

At first I was scared by the thought of a dog
Taking over my house, my room, my space
But she was so small, cuddly and a cute face.

She was as quiet as a mouse, but as playful as a kitten
I had to learn to live with her
I learned within a few weeks that she wasn't scary, just a puppy.

Casey is her name, so cute and soft
So playful and exciting
She needed so much care and attention
What if! What if! It was taken away from me.

Each time we took her out for a walk
She would hear a bus and she would start to shiver
So cute and cuddly
I just wish I could pick her up and cover her ears
But if I did she would never learn to live with them.

Amber Foreman (13)
Mackie Academy, Stonehaven

The Final Race But Just The Beginning

I climb aboard my sailing boat
I feel my breath catch in my throat
This is it, the final race
To gain my final finishing place

I sail towards the starting line
I pray that everything goes fine
The start gun goes off with a blast
And I pick up speed extremely fast

I close on the leaders with burning speed
I know I've just got to take the lead
I see one make a vital error
I'm going to give him a taste of terror

I pull along his starboard side
And he sails straight into the tide
He loses momentum and starts to fall back
I watch him falling right down the pack

I see the leader struggling up the beat
Now we're starting to feel the heat
I trick a tack and he goes to cover
No one can beat me which he will soon discover

He tacks back but he's now too late
It was always going to be his fate
Second place is not at all bad
But I am first which makes me glad

I cross the finish and I have won
But my sailing season has just begun
The 1st place trophy secures my place
In the Champion of Champions Worldwide Race.

Sean Tait (13)
Mackie Academy, Stonehaven

A Baby's On Its Way

I sat about nervously,
A baby was on its way.
Would I still get attention?
My life would change that day.

My nerves had turned to fear,
A baby is a pain,
Would my parents push me aside
Like a spider down the drain?

Then my dad came through the door,
His face was smiling foolishly,
'It's a girl,' he cried,
'Quickly, come and see.'

I saw her then, that's when I knew,
A baby is pure gold.
So small, so soft and delicate,
And light enough for me to hold.

Kirstin Leslie (13)
Mackie Academy, Stonehaven

Private Peaceful

I stand by my comrades
Not knowing if I or he will be there the next moment.
All I hear are screams of dying men
And the deafening sound of the hissing bombs
Sounding like screaming birds.
Before me the desolation of no-man's-land
Bodies of men lie motionless in empty craters
Briefly lit up by the crimson glare
The sharp-edged barbed wire stops my vision.
The shrill whistle of the bombs falling
Are heard above the patriotic cry
Of 'Go over the top!'
I must obey the command
Or pay the price with my life.

Jamie Carr (12)
McLaren High School, Callander

The Black Wolf

How majestic, how lonely, a wolf in the backdrop of the night.
Like a true hunter, he prowls in silence,
Eyes focused on his victim,
He stalks and strikes with great force.

His coat, soft to touch,
His eyes, amber,
Glowing in the dark, lighting his way
Through the patchy, star-lit forest.

His teeth are white as pearls,
Standing out from his perfect, black, velvet coat,
Like ripe berries on a thorny crown.

His body language is hard to understand,
Not just because he is an animal,
But because he's a lonely one,
And although he is alone he has many victories ahead.

He growls when he feels threatened
He yelps when hurt or scared.
His mixed emotions show he's unpredictable
And capable of putting up a scaring fight.

The way he moves, a slow intruder,
Pacing and treading with his feather-like steps,
And no matter how hard you may listen
You will never hear his flying approach.

The way he howls,
Is a supernatural gift.
Something he must use for reasons of his own.
To find a soulmate perhaps? Who knows?

All I know is, he's a hunter, a work of art,
A singer who likes the luminous moon, and of course,
A black wolf.

Laura MacDougall (12)
McLaren High School, Callander

My Auntie

I remember when I heard the news,
I was having fun in the sunlit garden,
My smile and laughter were gone,
For the news cut me like a knife.

I remember the suffering,
As if she had her own blunt sword and paper armour,
However hard she fought, it wasn't hard enough,
Illness kept coming. Illness upon illness,
Cancer, pneumonia and then the machines were brought in,
Finally came the sorrow, the heartache,
The end, the time of death had visited and left heavy laddered.

I remember the funeral,
It seemed the world was mourning along with us,
The clouds were heavy with grief,
Their tears spattering on the blackness and sadness all around,
The coffin was carried in, laden with flowers,
Pinned to the flowers were notes of grief and sorrow,
Like letters of farewell and blessing,
When we were praying, soft yet sad music played in the background,
I sneakily opened my eyes,
To this day I still wish I hadn't,
Light poured in the windows,
The curtains of the small inlet closed,
That was the last I ever saw of my aunt
The memory still hurts,
A wound that never heals.

Henrietta Bowie (12)
McLaren High School, Callander

Snap

I remember my first pony, Snap,
As an appealing cob,
She had a dominant chestnut coat that shone like the sun.
She was 13 hands high,
She had admirable brown eyes that had a twinkle in them.
When she jumped,
It felt like I was flying through the air.
She always cleared the jump.

Every time I rode her,
It felt like she was telling me something.
When she said whatever she said
I felt confident that we'd always be together.
But I was wrong.
We separated last year when she fell ill.
Her twinkle in her eyes had disappeared,
And her dominant chestnut colour in her coat
No longer shone like the sun,
I knew I was losing her.

It all happened one night, when I was at my local youth club,
My mum came to pick me up early,
And we drove down to Snap's stable,
It was then that my mum announced
That Snap was going to be put down,
When I heard this I hugged Snap as tight as I could,
Our whole time together flashed before me.
I still miss Snap and I always will,
But the most important thing is that she is still in my heart,
And no one can ever take that away from me.

Kirsten Innes (11)
McLaren High School, Callander

Black Arab

The icy wind in my hair
The tiny grains in my eyes
The hotness, the coldness
Of the sand.

I can hear water
But no water can be seen
The wilderness is a threatening world to be in
There is a dead tree
But no use to me

Then I see a stream
I run to see
I drink and drink and drink
And finally look up
To see a black Arab stallion
With his black flowing mane and small body
He is a colt with his short black tail
And has one white sock on his left front foot.

He takes me home
I give him water
But he snuffles with disinterest
I give him food
But no food he takes

I hug him and care for him
And what a relief
He eats and drinks
And loves the attention

One year later and I still have him
I hope to keep him for ever and ever.

Emma Buchanan (12)
McLaren High School, Callander

My Dog Jack

I am a dog
I have big feet
My favourite thing
To do is eat.

I like to jump
I like to play
But if I could
I'd run all day.

I fight my brother
I like to be tough
If we want food
It can be a bit rough.

I like a cuddle
I like a treat
But most of all
I love some meat.

My name is Jack
My fur is neat
If I were you
I'd think me sweet.

Morag O'Shaughnessy (12)
McLaren High School, Callander

The Guy In The Street

A homeless guy whines all the time
He scrambles in the street to find a dime
Though he has good reason to complain on his rug
Unless, it's his own fault for buying the drugs.

Sometimes he can never eat
Maybe not even for a week
But yet he lives on through the year
Until his death soon draws near.

Joshua McInnes (14)
McLaren High School, Callander

Panic Attack

Running
Hiding
All the things you do.
Anxious
Scared
All the things you feel.
Screaming
Shouting
All the things you hear.

No way out,
No way in,
Caught in the middle of nothing.
Just nothing,
Heart racing,
Blood pounding.

This is what happens in a *panic attack!*

Rachel Speirs (12)
McLaren High School, Callander

The Love

His starlit eyes brighten up her day
His golden hair, well, what's to say
His charm so great
Well, I must say, that's got to be fate

He looks at her with love
He sees her so high up above
He strokes her hand
He plays in a band

He says she's beautiful no matter what
He says this quite a lot
You know it's love
You know it's true
You know you want this to happen to you.

Sam Wallace (12)
McLaren High School, Callander

The Silly Fool

One day I was walking
Beside the bubbling brook,
Suddenly I spotted something moving
Upon inspection I saw a fish
A flash of gold and green
Circling and circling, darting and moving
I stared and stared in amazement
Got too close to the side
And fell in with a loud splash

People passing on their bikes
Laughed and laughed
What a sight!
I was dripping wet, miserable and cold
Walking home, my fishing net collapsed
My spirits crushed,
But my memory was alive and well.

Mathew Simpson (12)
McLaren High School, Callander

I Remember

I remember the strangeness
In Dad's tone as he called to us
I remember the stillness in the room
The almost unreal silence
Then feeling the shock
And pain of losing her
I remember the tears slipping
Down my cheeks and chin
Then I lost control
And the tears came gushing out
I remember the flowers
Laid upon her grave
And the unwanted realisation
That I'd lost her forever.

Corin Lang (12)
McLaren High School, Callander

Away With Imagination

She has a bag that's colourful with stars
She wants to take it up to Mars
Up in a rocket
It's rather drastic
Down with a crash
So she gets whiplash
She lands on a mountain
And drinks from a chocolate fountain
She rolls down the hill
That's where she meets Bill
They go to the river
It's so cold that they shiver
Then the girl goes home
And she sits all alone
Isolated and abandoned
Her mind still a whirr of possibilities
Eventually she goes to bed
Tucked up with her cuddly ted.

Hannah Petrie (12)
McLaren High School, Callander

The African War

I hear a distant rumble but nothing is there
The world is just a thick canopy of grass and trees
Then suddenly to interrupt the silence a Gatlin gun
Spits out hundreds of knives with a deadly rattle
Men fall all over like ants, a few shots were fired in vain
But they didn't even make a mark on the enemy
With the knife-like objects cutting through the flesh cruelly
I heard a wounded officer clutching his leg
Giving out orders, 'Retreat, retreat!'
I turned to run but just as I began I felt a prick hit my back
I fell into darkness
And joined those who fell that day, never to battle again.

Ross Thompson (11)
McLaren High School, Callander

Chocolate

Chocolate is my favourite thing
It makes me happy when I am down
It can be used for anything
Cakes, drinks, ice cream, to a plain bar
My favourite is the Crunchie
It melts in my mouth
And tingles on my tongue
It crunches and soothes
It runs through my teeth
Making holes as it goes along
But the bad thing is,
It makes you fat.

My second favourite is the Galaxy
I don't know why
But it is
It slips and slides
Down my chin like a waterslide
I just can't seem to get it in my mouth
I've really got to cut down on it
But it is like a drug you can't get enough of.

Nikki Fisher (12)
McLaren High School, Callander

The Man

I remember the man.
Face as white as chalk.
Frozen in a state of shock,
His skin all cold and waxy.

His eyes like huge goldfish bowls,
Pupils the size of fists.
His mouth hung open as if to say,
'Hey you, what's wrong with black!'

He lay as still as ice,
Starfished in a pool of blood.
And like a key to his heart,
A tiny hole pulsed red.

He did not move when a soundless ambulance drove up,
But carried on, on seeing the sight.

I question the world,
Again and again,
Why does racism have to exist?

Niamh Lee (11)
McLaren High School, Callander

Reflection

('For I do think she would not go into the awful place below' Marjory Fleming)

As Man does diminish into dust, what then for him?
Perhaps in heart a cherished flame; a murmur half-forgotten.
And what awaits him with the Rock: the key to all reason
                                                    and insanity;
Black night with its myriad of hopes extinguished;
                                    an unseen and futile truth.

Of those resigned to further strife
What lavish veil is laid before their eyes?
For can any man afford to buy their praise?
Yet would he oppose the sweep of common remembrance
Even if this were not so?

There still remains, in lessened magnitude,
A search and zeal for truth
Through which the cruel cold resolution of inexorable fashion
                                                    is endured.
Will an apostate of this expect apologia or kindly remembrance?

Tobias Shaw Paul (15)
McLaren High School, Callander

The Tree

There is a tree at the bottom of my garden,
It is as green as the canteen's beef curry.
The tree is very knobbly like a rock climber's wall,
The tree is so strong that I cannot fall.
The tree is fun to play on because of this,
I can sit on it all the day but when night comes,
I am sad to leave.
But hey, I can come back another day,
Sleep well my lovely tree, I will see you tomorrow.
Oh the tree and I have lived together all the time I have lived.
The tree never seems to not care
But when I don't say hello tree,
Or sit on it.
At night the tree goes away and goes to its tree friends
But they do not want to play.
So poor little tree goes back to the bottom of my garden
And it seems to weep.
But when morning comes and I go to it it is happy as can be.

James Gardner (12)
McLaren High School, Callander

The Secret Torture

Fear like a wound opens
As I leave the house
Been shaking all night
Steady now on the outside only

Stepping into the bus
Keeping my head down
The jeers rage around me
Like a hot, sharp wind
I cower in its midst
Why do they never really see me?

Stepping out, off the bus
I feel relieved
When I feel a hot sting
Something has pierced my skin
I fall to the ground
A foul dirty boot appears
It looms above me
Then another pain
Uncurls up my spine
I am alone
And committed
To my silence.

Adam Innes (13)
McLaren High School, Callander

Dirty Trainers

I have white shoes
With a blue tick
If you think yours are dirty
Then my trainers may seem sick
When I went out
With my friends
I went and slipped
Round a bend
There was a big tear
All I did was stare
My mum took one look
Then her shoulders shook,
'Those trainers are new,'
She said, turning blue.
'It wasn't my fault,'
I started to say
But she opened the door
And then threw them away
Now the sole of my shoes
A big size seven
Are floating on
To trainer Heaven.

Liam Garvie (12)
McLaren High School, Callander

War

The screams of men
The howling of bombs
The craters of shells
The burning of gas

The screech of bullets
And the crippled bodies
Is this war or is this *Hell?*

The clatter of guns
The thunder of planes
The fear of insanity
The loss of our loved ones

The crash of tanks
The bleeding of the wounded
All wars must not happen
But all wars must be *fought!*

Luke Melia (13)
McLaren High School, Callander

The Final Journey

I'm not alive but I'm not dead,
The silly thoughts that go through my head.
Lying here motionless day and night,
Life is brief, life is bright
Whether or not I must make farewells,
Trying not to cry, the sound of the bells.

I'm not angry, just feeling sad,
For all the bad times my family has had.
We've got each other though and that's worth more
Than that crazy driver I have no feelings for.

Well here's the doctor
You'd better be gone
Till then my friend
Please stay strong.

Lucy Brooks (13)
McLaren High School, Callander

War

The waiting
The tension
The cold
The fear
The waiting is over

The bombs
The fire
The screams
The bodies
The bombings are over

The retaliation
The gunfire
The enemy
The death
The war is over.

David McDonald (13)
McLaren High School, Callander

Theatre Of Dreams

Walking into the stadium, a red sea of fans,
Scarves raised and fluttering in anticipated triumph
Heart is thumping, blood pumping
The pitch shines like a sea of green
The kick-off is looming
The tension is rising,
A voice echoes throughout the stadium,
'Please welcome Manchester United and Chelsea.'
Emerging from the tunnel
Two rows of uniformed men
I can't believe it,
I see what is both familiar and new
I'm here at the Theatre of Dreams.

Scott Anderson (13)
McLaren High School, Callander

Paper

50% water
50% wood
Graphite, we call it lead,
Or use ink instead,
Carries the voice of the people.
Composed of lines,
From strong notes
To shades of colours,
Carries the feelings of people.

50% wood,
Wood equals power,
Paper carries power,
Trees are the origin of power,
Trees are our future.

David MacEachern (14)
McLaren High School, Callander

Homelessness

I am hungry and broke,
Poor as I can be,
Sitting with my cup at my side and my dog on my feet,
I've only earned a pound,
Just enough for a paper, a cup of tea
Drunk from a polystyrene cup.

Sitting on one of my newspapers,
Watching the world go by,
The people walk by, purposefully,

As self-contained as a sealed jar
Seeing them walking by, eating food and drinking drinks,
I feel my hunger
It gnaws like an animal and never leaves me.

Craig Campbell (13)
McLaren High School, Callander

Overlord

In the year of forty four
With the German Hun at our door
The allied men without fear or fright
Sailed into a deep dark night

They went through heavy seas and low cloud
But in the morning saw guns so loud
Onto the beach of blood and gore
Many thought, *so this is war*

For President, King not Queen
Most on the beach were aged nineteen
When they landed they were offensive
But for many hours were defensive

With all the blood, grit and sand
They won the day and pressed inland
They fought onward with saint or sin
With each campaign straight to Berlin.

Mark Devlin (12)
McLaren High School, Callander

My Passion

Horses, my passion,
Gorgeous and compassionate they are,
Their coats shining,
Even brighter than a star.

Though they are massive and full of power,
They can be very sweet and loving,
Like a friend,
They will always be there for you.

A horse is not just a racer or a pet,
For they will stick by you till the end,
A horse is something more,
Something better,
A best friend!

Maureen Kimuyu (13)
McLaren High School, Callander

The Season To Be Jolly?

It was Christmas night, we were hungry for tea
Mum couldn't come
She had to see Grandpa at the home, I don't know why
At the table Dad looked all tearful
But tried to cover it up by saying, 'Merry Christmas everyone.'
But we all knew something was wrong.
I thought I was dreaming, an uneasy Christmas
How could it be!
A very sad Christmas tea.
I went to bed
But I just couldn't sleep
Because on Boxing Day morning
The truth would start to seep.
As I expected it, of the declaring name
That name, 'Grandpa' put me to shame
The thought of him starting to die
Sent tears down my mind.
Seeing him smile at my lovely black dog
Made me shiver in the fog.
I think I am going to cry.

Robbie Oman (13)
McLaren High School, Callander

Sad Life

They call me names
Throw insults like sharp stones
It's not my fault
But they seem to make me
Feel more alone
I eat as comfort
Like dogs they pounce
I am dirt to them
Just because I am different

If I could stop eating I would
Be accepted
I feel my weight
Like a burden I cannot shift
It sets me apart
And the sharp edges
Of the insults go on

I wonder if I did stop eating
Would they treat me with respect?
If only they would see what is within
Rather than what is on the outside.

Andrew Orr (13)
McLaren High School, Callander

Gerri's Scarf

Gerri the giraffe,
Has a very long scarf,
With loads of bright colours,
Which she and her brothers
Argue over every day!
The scarf is so beautiful,
It makes her feel wonderful,
Then one gorgeous evening,
She found a better scarf,
Which she calls her bling!
So she gave her brothers,
Her old scarf with lots of bright colours,
Now she wears her bling,
Along with her golden ring!
In her happy zoo,
Where she relaxes with nothing to do!
Then along comes a child,
And starts to poke and prod,
She gets annoyed,
And starts to shake her head at Todd,
He grabs the end of her bling,
She pulls it back as if it's nothing,
Todd starts to bawl and shout,
And ends up with nowt!

Brooklyn Bell (12)
McLaren High School, Callander

Stranger

My trouble begins . . .

Everyone seems against me,
I am a stranger,
I have been mocked and laughed at,
When we first arrived I felt small and vulnerable.
I was alone.
I left all my friends,
And all my confidence along with them.

Everyone digs at the first chance they get,
Their insults and jeers
Are thrown like missiles
I am alone.
My accent and trends are different.
I am a stranger.

People look at me as I walk
Down the stark, electric lit corridor
I hear them whisper behind my back.
Muted curses, laughter like crystal.

Acceptance will come,
Acceptance will come.

William Vernon (13)
McLaren High School, Callander

My View

As I sit in my chair
Listening to the world I cannot see
I feel the faithful dog that sits by my side
All fluffy and soft, sitting beside me
I imagine her gazing up at me with sad faithful eyes
Without her I would be lost in the world I cannot see
Every day she acts as my eyes for me
Her patience as she waits for cars to pass by
Her loving nature as children stop to say hello
Flopping down at my bedside at night
Never wandering far from my side in case I need her
The only one in the world that truly loves me
Never whispering about me behind my back
Never hurting my feelings
I am faithful to her
She is faithful to me
My oldest friend now dying
Am I betraying her by getting this new dog?
But she seems to understand she is dying
Refusing to die until she is sure this dog will care for me
Then she gives her final yelp as if to say goodbye
Then her chest ceases to rise and fall in its steady rhythm
And with my hand against her I feel her heart slow down and stop
I feel the tears welling up and choking me in the back of my throat
I gently kiss her on the nose and whisper goodbye
To the friend that's treated me so well
Goodbye I will miss you.

Kaleidh Bruce (13)
McLaren High School, Callander

Football

As I stand in the tunnel,
Waiting to lead the team out,
It's cold and you can feel the tension,
The teams start to move onto the pitch,
With my favourite player beside me,
The noise starts to build up as I run out,
I can see all the fans cheering as I look up to the stands,
I am in the centre circle getting my photo taken,
I shake hands with the ref and the Rangers captain,
As I run off the pitch the Dunfermline captain calls me back,
He shouts, 'I'll score a goal for you!'
As he sticks his thumb up,
The whistle blew for the kick-off,
Full-time,
We won the game 2-0,
It was the first time we'd beaten Rangers in the league,
History had been made.

Christopher Addison (13)
McLaren High School, Callander

The Meanings Of Rain

Rain can be a precious thing,
The water smashing on the ground.
It is like a bomb,
Smashing,
Crashing,
Hitting the ground,
But also it can be so delicate,
Dainty,
Exquisite
And making the meticulous and quietest little sound.

But to people it can be a thing of hatred,
Detestable and repulsive.
The dampness can really get to people,
And sometimes rain can remind people of tears.

Some people put down rain
Because of the dark, cheerless clouds.
Some people wish that if they could
They would grab rain and put it in the bin.

Amie Duffy (13)
McLaren High School, Callander

Life

Life is just like one big film
A bit of action
A little romance
But more sadness

No matter how happy you are
Something gets you down
A joke makes you laugh
The taxman takes it away

You work for a living
To stay alive
Enjoy the good things in life
But someone has to spoil it

It's not really worth it
Jokes are great
Friends are the best
But death can be a relief.

James McBeath (13)
McLaren High School, Callander

Golden Beach

Golden beach, bustling metropolis.
Sand dunes and blue sea.
Heatwave is unbearable, ice cream selling very fast.
Little kids bounding around.
Old people lazing about,
Little wind, high sun,
Beautiful waves hit the sand.
Golden sun shines above.

Grey beach, ghost town.
Giant grey monstrous waves,
So cold, so cold.
Little kids wrapped up warm,
Old folk stay indoors.
Horrible winter, horrible beach.

James O'Lone (14)
Nendrum College, Comber

Icicles

Icicles like see-through bats hanging from rooftops,
The frozen snow, like fairy wands dangling all around,
Waiting for the sun to put them to bed.
She comes out and gently they fall to the ground.

The thawing snow is dripping,
But as day turns into night
The temperature is at freezing,
Icicles shine brightly in the moonlight.

They shiver and shake in the peaceful night,
'Til morning awakens a brand new day.
The sun rises high and warm in the sky,
Startled icicles melt quickly in her warm sunny ray.

The cycle repeats day after day,
The seasons exchange, a winter for spring.
We patiently wait for another new year,
Once again to hear the icicles sing.

Charlotte Walker (11)
Nendrum College, Comber

Christmas Morning

She wakes from her bed,
Things swirling through her head.
Running down the stairs,
She spies some teddy bears.
Then she hears some rustling
And some fistiling and fustling,
It's coming from the tree.
'Is it for me?'
Two bright eyes,
A wagging tail,
'I think I'll call her Abigail.'

Codie Nisbet (12)
Nendrum College, Comber

Nativity In 20 Seconds

Silent night
Candlelight
Holly bright

Stable poor
Prickly straw
Donkey snore

Babe asleep
Lambs leap
Shepherds peep

Star guide
Kings ride
Manger side

Angels' wings
Bells ring
Children sing
Welcome King.

Aaron English (14)
Nendrum College, Comber

My Area

The morning mist
Covers the fields like a blanket,
Eerie shadows of sheep emerge from the gloom.
Trees like statues stand in the mist
Waving their arms from side to side,
Waiting for the sun to creep
From behind the hill.
The mist rolls away
Revealing the country
In all its glory.
The shadows disappear
And the trees come alive,
But the world still goes on.

Ruth Barr (14)
Nendrum College, Comber

I Am . . .

I am a fashion model,
Walking into the room and holding a pose,
Cameras flashing and people throwing roses at me,
Fans admiring the sparkly dress that I am wearing.

I am an animal rescuer,
Holding onto the net which is going down the narrow hole to rescue

a lion cub,
On my way back I stop and let the cub join the pride.

I am the newest pop star,
Coming into the gigantic stadium, fans screaming and singing,
TV cameras taping me on live television.

I am a show jumper,
Starting the course.
As I enter the ring the audience applaud as I leap over the jumps,
When I get my trophy I am very happy.

I am Cassie Gilliland,
Year 8, good at music,
I love to sing and play instruments,
Blonde hair, blue eyes, I go to Nendrum College, Comber.

Cassie Gilliland (11)
Nendrum College, Comber

My Little Sister

I love the way she gives me a cuddle and kiss at night.
I love the way she play with her dolls.
I love the way she hugs me tight.
I love the way she laughs when she falls.

I dislike the way she pretends to be a baby,
Or when she gets under my feet.
I dislike the way she snores,
Or annoys me when my friends and I meet.

Her favourite colour is blue
And she loves to swim in the sea.
Her favourite clothing is a shoe
And she loves to hang out with me.

Her eyes are the truest of blue,
Her hair is shiny and dark.
She will surely seem cute to you,
She will always melt your heart.

This is why I love her,
For surely I do.
She's the best little sister,
I'm sure you'll think so too!

Rebecca Woods (14)
Nendrum College, Comber

The Beach

Soft, glittery sand,
Trapped in my hand,
Hot blazing sun,
The fun has only begun,
Tropical ocean breeze,
My bucket is going to freeze,
Splashing, roaring waves,
Tanned sunbathers bathe,
Big, beautiful sandcastles,
Seashells admire and dazzle,
Tangles of seaweed,
Poke it with a reed,
Watching the beach boys is a pleasure,
Digging for buried treasure,
Cool strawberry ice cream,
The children all beam.

Kendal Jowett (13)
Nendrum College, Comber

My Area

Lying in the golden sand,
Swimming in the glinting sea,
Soaking up the sun,
Fishermen fishing off the rocky cliffs,
Watching yachts sail by,
Swimming after speedy fish,
Watch the crabs march across the sand,
Get covered in suncream,
Lying on the towels,
Surfing on a surfboard,
Playing with a beach ball,
Trying to avoid the sun,
Sweating in the intense heat,
Lying in the golden sand.

Ryan Craig (14)
Nendrum College, Comber

I Like . . .

Poor people need it
Rich people give it
Money
I like that stuff

Some people love it
Lots of people wear it
Clothes
I like that stuff

People like the smell of it
People like to dream of it
Food
I like that stuff

People like to swim in it
People like a drink of it
Water
I like that stuff.

Chloe Brown (11)
Nendrum College, Comber

Summer City

Warm city. Warm city
Fast rising heat is furious
Cars crawl, to try and find the shade
The icy blue sky
High above the hot
Metal frames of the swings
People more like robots
As they walk home
From work and school
Children run about shouting
Singing while their parents sit
Inside their homes drinking
Ice cool fruit cocktails.

Thom Hinds (14)
Nendrum College, Comber

Snowflakes

Snowflakes are falling
Everywhere,
Falling to the ground
Without a sound.
At the stroke of midnight
Everything goes quiet,
Children are sleeping, dreaming
Of all the toys they will receive
In the morning.
The ground slowly dusts
With snow.
Rooftops that were black
Turn to white.
Windowsills become covered,
Cars all white.
Snowflakes are silent,
They don't make a sound
As they fall
        to
          the
            ground.

Emma McManus (13)
Nendrum College, Comber

Christmas

The crimson red berries on the holly,
'Ho ho ho,' shouts Santa all jolly,
One whistle to his reindeer and off they all go,
It falls and falls, more and more snow,
Christmas lights everywhere like stars in the sky,
I scoffed three steaming-hot mince pies,
The angel sits high on the Christmas tree,
Women go wild on their Christmas shopping spree,
Everyone celebrating with wine and beer,
Not long now until the New Year.

Stephen Reid (14)
Nendrum College, Comber

My Ghostly Neighbourhood

Ghostly, dull, graffiti-covered neighbourhood,
Hooligans' playground and filth heaven.
Glass bottles like traps glisten in the dark,
Newspaper covers the ground like carpet.
Graffiti artists send messages that cry out,
Dull cars reflect street light.
Dastardly drains running quickly,
Teenagers trudge home recently.
All hoodlums are despised,
Every telephone box is vandalised.
Children crouch in houses afraid to go out,
Pensioners lock their doors and windows.
Ghostly, dull, graffiti-covered neighbourhood,
Ghostly, dull, graffiti-covered neighbourhood.

Martin Ferguson (13)
Nendrum College, Comber

My Street At Night

Greyness stretches for miles
Cats shriek like banshees
Purr of a motorbike
Gentle din of distant chatter echoes eerily
Red fox on the prowl
The river gently flows
Car lights twinkling in the distance
Dogs are barking wildly
Stars sparkle in the sky
Street lights flame like orange beach balls
A plane flies overhead
The night goes on
The moon gets bigger
Greyness stretches for miles.

Emma Crawford (14)
Nendrum College, Comber

I Like . . .

Children play with it
Angels are made with it
Snow
I like that stuff

People dance to it
Poetry is made with it
Music
I like that stuff

Happiness is made of it
Families share it
Love
I like that stuff

Life and freedom is found in it
Nations live in it
Earth
I like that stuff.

Hannah Elizabeth Cash (11)
Nendrum College, Comber

A Christmas Poem

We celebrate and put tinsel on a tree,
Wrapped presents on the floor.
The bee is gone from summertime,
Garland wrapped around the door.

Mistletoe hanging above our eyes,
Santa singing, 'Ho! Ho! Ho!'
Winter when the flowers die,
My brother going, 'No! No! No!'

Jesus' birthday, hip hip hooray,
Holly hanging on the door.
I wonder what age He is today,
Tinsel touching the floor.

Connor Lynn (12)
Nendrum College, Comber

I Like That Stuff

People play it
Fans watch it
Football
I like that stuff

People listen to it
50 Cent makes it
Music
I like that stuff

Everyone has them
You can't live without them
Friends
I like that stuff

Everyone goes on them
You have a good time on them
Holidays
I like that stuff.

Jason Cromie (12)
Nendrum College, Comber

I Am . . .

I am a footballer skinning defenders inside out,
Having a shot and hoping to score.

I am a ten pin bowler bowling the ball
Watching it swerve about then getting a strike.

I am a tree shooting high in the sky.
Children climb me and birds nest on me.

I am a race car driver revving the car
Reaching speeds of 130mph in the Grand Prix.

I am Jordan Spencer, good at maths, OK at English,
Must work hard.

Jordan Spencer (11)
Nendrum College, Comber

The Funfair

With your money all ready,
The long queues await,
All screams echo round the field,
Balloons flying round in the sky
That the little ones have let go of.

People's hearts are jumping in tune,
To the very loud music,
Plastic bags blowing everywhere
And glass bottles break.

Lots of prizes being won,
But the best prize to win is
The gigantic cuddly teddy.

The fluffy pink candyfloss
Melts in your mouth,
Sweet papers blow along the ground
As well as the drink cans,
But the best bit is all
The fun, breathtaking rides.

Aimee Orr (14)
Nendrum College, Comber

Christmas Nights

T insel wrapped tight round the tree
R udolph racing through the sky
E verything quiet like a mouse
E verything lies still till Santa comes

S nowmen wrapped in wool and cotton
A nd snowballs flying through the sky
N ight-time falls, not long now till Santa comes
T ea time comes and goes
A s my excitement gets the hold of me.

Samantha Craigan (11)
Nendrum College, Comber

I Like That Stuff

Red roses lying on the floor,
Getting cards through my door,
Valentine's Day,
I like that stuff.

Getting presents on that day
And getting my friends over to stay,
My birthday,
I like that stuff.

Strutting my moves across the floor,
I love entering through the stage door,
Dancing,
I like that stuff.

By day it's lovely, warm and bright,
But it goes to sleep during the night,
The sun,
I like that stuff.

Megan Stevenson (12)
Nendrum College, Comber

I Am . . .

I am a fish swimming in the sea, eating green plants,
digging down in the coral.

I am a vet helping different animals, going on the trips
to different countries, helping wild animals.

I am a tiger jumping on the trees, playing with different tigers,
catching wild animals.

I am an interior designer designing houses for people,
selling them to different countries.

I am Justyna Panas, class 8P, I don't really like school
And I like shopping.

Justyna Panas (12)
Nendrum College, Comber

I Am . . .

I am the first woman astronaut
Shooting up in the rocket, space
Walking on every planet, meeting
Aliens as I walk past them, collecting
Pieces of sparkling rocks and catching
Stars in my hands as they float in mid-air.

I am an artist dipping my paintbrush into
My paint tray and discovering new colours
For my pictures.

I am an ice skater coming in the ice rink,
Dancing and doing jumps and spins, making
A trail as I skate with the audience
Screaming and cheering.

I am a musician playing my guitar full blast with
My band, singing through the microphone,
Spotlights on me and audience waving at me
And wanting my autograph.

I am Ashleigh McQueen, 8P, likes art and dancing.

Ashleigh McQueen (12)
Nendrum College, Comber

I Am . . .

I am an Olympic ice skater, purple and sparkly,
swishing on the ice.

I am a golfer, stripy and smartly dressed,
feeling the breeze and winning a putt.

I am the ten pin bowler, flat shoed and fast,
making a strike.

I am a piano player, concentrating,
playing merrily.

I am Laura McMillan, class 8P, music lover,
good at English, need to keep up good work.

Laura McMillan (12)
Nendrum College, Comber

I Am . . .

I am Thierry Henry weaving in and out of the defenders
past one, past two, past three, ready to shoot and score a goal.

I am an alien in my UFO blasting people with my laser gun
protecting the universe from the other aliens.

I am Michael Schumacher going at 250 mph
round the German race track overtaking all the other racers
and winning the German Grand Prix.

I am a brave warrior, ready to kill the evil barbarian army
with my mighty Roman soldiers also ready to kill.

I am Andrew, good at football and maths
and I play for Comber Rec Football Club.

Andrew McClure (11)
Nendrum College, Comber

I Am . . .

I am a fish exploring the deep blue sea, digging down in the coral,
swimming away from the dangerous sharks!

I am an actress singing and dancing, saying my words
as the audience sits in amazement.

I am a tree growing as high as I possibly can,
letting people from below climb up my long trunk
as the wind blows my leaves.

I am a lottery winner, excited and tense, to feel the excitement
of my numbers being called out and to have a big house!

I am Danielle Toman, slow at maths, good at English,
must concentrate on my work.

Danielle Toman (12)
Nendrum College, Comber

I Like . . .

I am never alone when I go outside,
Because they are always by my side.
Friends,
I like that stuff.

They are black and white and have a beak
And sometimes they make an annoying squeak.
Penguins,
I like that stuff.

When my legs move fast,
I feel a windy blast.
Running,
I like that stuff.

You sometimes lie flat
And sometimes curl up like a cat.
Bed,
I like that stuff.

This musical instrument is hard to blow
And sometimes it sounds like a crow.
Flute,
I like that stuff.

They are yellow and funny
And make me laugh from my tummy.
The Simpsons,
I like that stuff.

Benjamin English (11)
Nendrum College, Comber

I Like . . .

They keep me happy
We have fun together
Friends
I like that stuff

It's hard to play
You need great breath
Bagpipes
I like that stuff

It keeps you warm
You feel cosy in it
Bed
I like that stuff

Footballers play with it
Liverpool won the cup with it
Football
I like that stuff.

Travis Heaybourne (12)
Nendrum College, Comber

I Am . . .

I am a famous showjumper flying over the massive jumps,
cantering over to the jump, lifting up in the air, waiting to hear
the sound of hooves landing on the ground from mid-air.

I am a millionaire living in a boiling country, swimming in
the deep, dark blue water in my back garden, my maids
standing waiting for me to get out with my towel and my drink.

I am a pop star, people cheering my name to come on to the stage,
making hundreds of CDs and signing people's T-shirts.

I am a famous dressmaker, my customers waiting
for the shop to open, making millions every day.

I am Rebecca Gibson, love dancing, good at maths,
need to work hard at English and in my schoolwork.

Rebecca Gibson (12)
Nendrum College, Comber

I Am

I am the Doctor's assistant, flying in the TARDIS,
seeing the future before it comes.

I am Hermione Granger, on my broomstick,
the feeling of the wind in my hair,
escaping the Muggle world by port-key.

I am a meerkat sunning my back in the hot Kalahari sun,
looking for eagles in the sky,
letting out warring calls when the time is right.

I am Sharpy from 'High School Musical',
singing the best songs in the winter musical,
wearing the best clothes in the school.
When I say quiet everyone is silent.

I am Toni-Lee Martin, slow at RE, good at history;
I must concentrate on my work.

Toni-Lee Martin   (12)
Nendrum College, Comber

Blind Man

I was walking one day and saw a blind man trying to cross the road.
It hurt me inside that people should ignore him; no one even tried

He stood on the pavement alone, afraid
Not a single person came to his aid

Instead they pushed by as if they were blind too
They just didn't care how he must feel

I couldn't remain there watching him standing
I went over to help him out of his trouble

I've learned from St Christopher's to help and to care
From all of the people who have helped me there
So off I went and helped that blind man
I like to think I will help when I can
I think more people should care in the community
It would make our town a nicer place to be.

Elin Rennard
St Christopher's School, Wrexham

Halfway To A Dream

I was unwanted; Mum couldn't care less.
I was a child whose life was a mess.
I felt such hurt, nevertheless
No one was there to share my distress.

I was unfed and not even clean.
At school I was teased which really was mean.
No children wanted me in their team.
I was not part of anyone's scheme.

Life changed at the age of eight, one rainy day
When social services took me away.
In foster care I could go out to play.
But nothing will take the pain away.

The years have passed; I've reached seventeen.
I'm now well fed and I keep very clean.
At St Christopher's school no one is mean.
I have friends aplenty and the entire staff team
Do their best to make me realise my dream.

That dream is to live in a loving family.
Not much to most people but the world to me.

Karen Shone (17)
St Christopher's School, Wrexham

My Best Friend

I never feel down because I've got my best friend,
Bob will stand by me to the bitter end,
He'll always cheer me when I'm down,
He'll always be there when I frown,
Even when I feel deluded,
I know I'll never feel excluded.

Jamie Roberts (14)
St Christopher's School, Wrexham

The People Within

They may look old and complain of the cold
But herein lies a story that needs to be told
My nan and taid mean the world to me
And play a major part in my family

They have always been there since I was small
And I love them so much, warts and all
Their hair is grey and falling out
And people stare as they walk about

I wish these people I see stare, laugh and joke
Would see the people they are inside, instead of decrepit old folk
They call them grumpy and say that they stink
I wish these people could just stop and think

For although they move so slow and are weak and frail
And unusual to look at with their memories starting to fail
But over the years some stories they've told
Which will live in my memory until I myself grow old

All these two wonderful people have ever shown me is true love
And I understand that not long from now they are destined for
                                        Heaven above
So society must stop, think and show more care
And make them feel wanted and special before they get there

Because when they've gone it will be too late
So it's time to put an end to this ridicule and hate
And accept these dear old folk just as people
As they are merely you and I in the future and should be treated
                                        as equals.

Daniel Walker
St Christopher's School, Wrexham

Neglected

It was on the news I saw them one day,
Neglected children crying away.

They'd been dumped by their parents and left all alone,
Found in boxes and binbags, chilled to the bone.

It tore at my heart to see them like this,
I wanted to reach out and give them a kiss.

A little girl lying alone in a cot,
Kicking and screaming but who gives a jot.

Someone approached her, a scowl on their face,
They lifted their hand with a cruel grimace.

She cried out aloud in terrible pain,
But the blows rained down again and again.

I wanted to stop the evil I saw,
I got up to go, what more could I do?

Then up came a thought of things I could do,
To help get these children out of this zoo.

They first needed money to give them a chance
And leave the terrible place far in the distance.

I gave them some money, other people did too,
The chance of freeing them grew and grew.

Then came the news I'd been awaiting so long,
The children were free from a life so, so wrong.

Jamie Lee Morgan (16)
St Christopher's School, Wrexham

Why, Oh Why

Why, oh why do they have to suffer,
their lives bad enough and getting rougher?

Without a thought people stand and stare,
and others pass by as though they are not there;

What have they done to be treated this way,
to fight and struggle to get through the day?

Their tears, their cries and their life of woe,
God only knows it shouldn't be so.

Why, oh why don't we all understand,
in this so-called civilised land?

They may look different, but they've still got a soul,
is it not possible to make them whole?

All deserve a chance no matter their needs,
forget their problems, their colour, their creeds;

They are all human, of that we are sure,
and yet there are those who would deny them more.

Delwyn Challoner (15)
St Christopher's School, Wrexham

Anti-Bullying

Bullying is nasty and it's disgusting.
People bully because they think they are hard.
Until they are on their own.

When they are on their own they are quiet
And walk past with their heads down,
Until they are back with their gang.

Dean Kinsella
St Christopher's School, Wrexham

Inclusion

I am in the Kop with all my mates,
We sing our songs all dressed in red,
We look out for each other,
We laugh together,
We cry with each other,
We play fight with each other,
We sing songs together,
We run around and jump up and down when the team score,
Everyone is included, it's pure inclusion.

My friend and I were dressed in red,
We walked through our rivals' city centre,
Twenty boys in blue came towards us,
There were only two of us,
We felt scared,
We were worried,
We felt like running in different directions,
We felt like they were coming for us,
The ultimate exclusion.

James Thomas (15)
St Christopher's School, Wrexham

Falling Out

I fell out with my friend at school,
He'd made me look a fool.

It made me feel sad,
It made me feel mad,
It made me think,
What did I do wrong?

The next day we spoke together.
Friends forever,
It filled me with glee,
Happy as could be,
Included.

Gavin Ansonia (14)
St Christopher's School, Wrexham

You

I like your eyes
I like your smile
I adore your ways
I cherish your style
You're one of a kind
You are always on my mind
I'm glad to be included in your world.

I hate your eyes
I hate your smile
I hate your ways
I hate your style
What can I say
You were one of a kind
On my mind
I'm excluded.

Ian Owen (15)
St Christopher's School, Wrexham

Inclusion

I feel happy
I feel glad
I feel wanted
I feel special
I feel good
I feel included.

Tommy Doran (15)
St Christopher's School, Wrexham

The Day She Went

The day she went,
I thought my family was going to end,

The day she went,
I thought I would be on my own forever,

The day she went,
I had a huge hole in my heart,

The day she went,
I thought I would break apart.

A year now has passed since the day she went.

I still feel that she is with me,

We are more of a family than ever before,

We will always be together, she's fixed the hole in my heart.

One thing is for sure, now we will never be apart.

Chanice Owen-Jones (14)
St Christopher's School, Wrexham

Inclusion

Inclusion is respect for everyone,
Inclusion is participation,
Inclusion is someone to talk to,
Inclusion is someone to talk with,
Inclusion is when we look out for each other.

Peter Wheeler (14)
St Christopher's School, Wrexham

The World

I wish people would listen
I'm getting hotter
I'm using my skin
I'm sweating immensely

I have a cold
I have a runny nose
Ice caps are melting
What will happen, nobody knows

I have a headache
And a cold
I think it's from all the smoke
I'm inhaling in

My hairs are falling down and off
There is a hole in my head
I'm dying
I am the Earth.

Calum Ryan (11)
Ysgol Bryn Elian, Colwyn Bay

In The Night

I roam around in the darkest night
Waiting for the moon to shine bright
I sprout some hair, I start to howl
The dogs nearby start to growl
When people see me they freeze and stare
I go to chase, but they run screaming in despair
I stop running and sit alone
And wonder why I'm on my own.

Abigail Rollinson (16)
Ysgol Bryn Elian, Colwyn Bay

Aliens And The Earth

In the aliens' spacecraft,
The aliens don't have fun.
There is terrible, dreadful news,
That the global warming's begun.

They say it's all the humans' fault,
With all that litter around.
Polluting the sea, polluting the Earth,
Polluting the air in the town.

So the aliens decide to do something,
To teach those silly humans.
They will send in fire, wind and tornadoes
To stop the humans' doings.

In the end there's ice and snow,
Scattered across the Earth.
The aliens give us one more chance,
As a new human gives birth.

In the aliens' spacecraft,
The aliens don't have fun.
There is terrible, dreadful news,
That the global warming's begun.

James Davies (11)
Ysgol Bryn Elian, Colwyn Bay

Runescape, The PC Game

R avishing through the wilderness, fighting side by side
U nable to destroy, I find a way to escape
N ow I see that 982,000 people are playing
E ven if I want 1000k, but I have to live with what I got
S o I find a box of destructive weapons
C alling a demon, I slayed it by dawn
A nd all the people of Varrock
P raised me by giving me bark
E ven if this game is addictive, it's still fun.

Daniel Thomas (11)
Ysgol Bryn Elian, Colwyn Bay

A Dog's Tale!

I had a happy life,
I had doggy treats and a bed,
I even had a doggy wife,
Now she is dead and I've lost my bed.

They tied me up and hit me,
Then they threw me in the dump,
It was only a little pee,
But that made them worse, *thump, thump, thump.*

I shiver and yelp,
But no one is there,
I need some help,
Will someone answer my prayer?

I am hungry and cold,
I am forced to eat mould,
I have to or I will die,
Why! Oh why! Oh why!

I had a happy life,
I had doggy treats and a bed,
I even had a doggy wife,
Now she is dead and I have forever lost my bed.

Kora Hardern-Riley (11)
Ysgol Bryn Elian, Colwyn Bay

Terror 9/11

It's like the end of the world . . .
With nothing to see
At the end of it all
The air is so thick and the skies are so black
We panic
There's no looking back
And our hearts race
Out of control
And we cry
Because we can't go home
This ain't the place I know
Taste the fear in their dying breaths
The glass breaks and the ash flies
The screams
They haunt the crowds
It's someone's fault
Whether it's them or us
It caved in on their hearts
It caved in on their dreams
It caved in on their hope
It broke the promised peace . . .
All I know is death must be an honour and a gift
To those who bring it

Michael Zachariah Storm Rogers (16)
Ysgol Bryn Elian, Colwyn Bay

A Baby's Day!

They watch me all day long,
Singing sweet gentle songs,
It makes me cry even more
And that really does make my mouth sore!

They must know what it could be,
All day I've been waiting to see,
Just what exactly lies in my nappy?
If you change it I'll be so happy!

They always try and make me laugh,
But most of the time it's just naff.
She sits and sips her tea
And props me on her knee.

She lays me on my mat,
Takes off my coat and hat,
But it's very, very cold,
I want somebody to hold.

She picks me up and holds me tight
And turns me round into the light,
I'm tired now I want to sleep,
But Daddy's outside in the car, *beep beep!*

Antonette Christie (11)
Ysgol Bryn Elian, Colwyn Bay

If I Were A Bird

If I were a bird I'd fly from branch to branch,
Watching a horse run on a hot summer's ranch.

If I were a bird I'd fly from place to place,
Flying over countries with people of a different race.

If I were a bird I'd help people to see,
What a wonderful place the world can be.

Help them to see peace and help them see love
And to see what it's like for a bird up above.

Abbie Joyce (16)
Ysgol Bryn Elian, Colwyn Bay

Teenagers

As I stand with my crowd of friends,
I see a group of ladies.
They walk past and glare and stare,
I hear words I cannot bear.

As I look on with my friends,
I see another crowd.
They swear and chant and frighten those,
Who stand their ground and strike a pose.

But it's not fair as I stare,
To class us all the same.
Life is short, it should be lived,
We should put the thugs to shame.

My friends and I are full of care,
To see louts stop and stare.
They should be sent away to work,
Instead of causing hatred while they smirk.

They seem obsessed to frighten those,
With their hoodies and their bows.
We should all help in times like this,
To show them that they won't be missed.

Heidi Ellis (11)
Ysgol Bryn Elian, Colwyn Bay

Friends

F orever friends
R ely on the latest trends
I will always love them
E ven though they drive me round the bend
N ever-ending love
D oing anything for them
S till my friends till the end.

Becky Morgans (15)
Ysgol Bryn Elian, Colwyn Bay

Jade Goody

My life is really bad,
I feel so sad,
I don't know what I did,
I was acting like a little kid.

You see my face on the TV,
I'm not treated the way I used to be,
Inside I feel all alone,
All everybody does is moan.

I do the best for my boys,
I try to give them lots of toys,
I don't know what is going wrong,
I'm all alone and not strong.

I got voted off for giving grief,
What I said was not in my real belief,
I've been called all sorts of names,
I'm now just losing fame!

Kayleigh Griffiths (11)
Ysgol Bryn Elian, Colwyn Bay

Dogs For Life

D ry, wet, fluffy and smooth
O r playful, loyal and ready to groove
G rooming, walking and feeding
S o they are very needing!

For

L ife is not just for Crimbo
I t's all the time you bimbo!
F ood, bowl and grooming glove
E very day they need these, but mostly they need *love!*

Charlotte Stephenson (11)
Ysgol Bryn Elian, Colwyn Bay

A Dog's Life

They wake me up with all the noise,
It's probably the rattling of toys,
I'm hungry now, I want some food,
They've really put me in a mood.

I really want a big juicy bone,
Why have they left me all alone?
I'm now awake and in my bed,
I'm sitting up, waiting to be fed.

I can hear the baby crying,
If I said I cared then I'd be lying,
If I cried would they care about me?
I'll have to try it and wait and see.

She picks the tiny toddler up
And feeds him milk from a cup,
She rests him down and looks my way,
She does this to me every day!

If they ever bothered to take me out
And just let me have a run about,
If only I had all that love,
Maybe just a little hug.

I know he's young and very small,
But does that make a difference at all?
What is all this hatred for?
I may as well walk out the door.

Chloé Rowlands (11)
Ysgol Bryn Elian, Colwyn Bay

Racing Horse

At the start line
Ready to go
On my hooves
My jockey's getting ready and low

The gunshot blows
And off I trot
The whip hits my back
And it hurts a lot

Getting halfway
Round the track
I'm coming second
First is Big Mack

Chasing her
On her tail
Trying to overtake
This can't fail

Still coming in second
Staring at the finish line
I'm getting whipped hard
I let out a whine

It's getting closer
Here it is
Running my heart out
I'm like a whiz

Whipping harder
Running faster
As I go and
Pass her

Over the line
I'm only a beginner
I claim my jockey and me
The winner.

Becky Heap (14)
Ysgol Bryn Elian, Colwyn Bay

The Earth

The Earth is unwell
The Earth is very sick
The Earth is left wondering
How mankind could be so thick

How could mankind
Just come wandering in
Turning the beautiful Earth
Into a rubbish bin?

Why did mankind
Make loads of smoke
Burning through the ozone layer
Because this is just a joke?

Mankind got onto Earth
Like nits get into hair
Ruining its beauty
And that just isn't fair

The Earth is unwell
The Earth is very sick
The Earth is left wondering
How mankind could be so sick.

Kieran Jones (13)
Ysgol Bryn Elian, Colwyn Bay

Friends

F un to be around
R andomly running around
I rrelevant matters discussed
E njoying the company
N o one cares what you do
D oing loads of silly things
S creaming louder and louder.

Nicholas Carter (15)
Ysgol Bryn Elian, Colwyn Bay

Liverpool FC

The grass is good,
The weather's fine, in 10 minutes
I'm about to shine.

Whistle blows, adrenalin kicks in,
The FA Cup is ours to win.

United kick off the crowd roars wild,
Steve G runs down the field whips in a cross
For Pennant to seal,
We're 1-0 up, United are stuck.

At half-time we're playing well but then
United strike as well.

The game's 1-1, Steve G is the one,
He strikes the ball from 31,
What a great goal with 5 mins left,
Surely the cup is Liverpool's.

1 min left, United break, Rooney strikes,
It hits the side net with Reina looking worried.

Liverpool win for the 8th time,
Gerrard thinking, *thank God it's mine.*

Adam Mottram
Ysgol Bryn Elian, Colwyn Bay

Cruelty

I am a dog who's lonely and cold
I live by a river, as I am very old
I got thrown out by my owner
Who was a very old loner

I am made up of colours
Black, brown and white
As I sparkle in the light
Of a freezing cold night

I am very hungry, as I can't eat
I do get beaten for my meat
As I walk past people I cower and shiver
I am scared to look up as they make me quiver.

*(The moral of this poem is: respect animals,
Animals are for life not just for Christmas.)*

Bethany Ellis (11)
Ysgol Bryn Elian, Colwyn Bay

Rio Ferdinand

Rio lived on the Friary Estate in Peckham
He is now compared to
The likes of Ronaldo and Beckham

He started his football career at West Ham
I'm his number one fan

He then played for Leeds
He has done many good deeds

He then played for Man U
Alex knew he could do almost anything.

Sam Durrans (12)
Ysgol Bryn Elian, Colwyn Bay

Thumper Star

There once was a rabbit,
He had a bit of a habit,
Like chewing up the edge of a drawer,
Or urinating all over the floor,
What a naughty rabbit!

The rabbit's name was Thumper,
He was one heck of a jumper,
When he dived over the garden wall,
He used the neighbour to break his fall,
Sadly there was no shelter, not even a bunker!

Carrots were his favourite nibble,
Asparagus just made him wriggle,
Basketball was his delight,
You should have seen him in full flight,
Shooting hoops made him giggle,
Like Michael Jordan, he could dribble!

Jake Clutton (13)
Ysgol Bryn Elian, Colwyn Bay

That Horrid Bully

I am in the playground,
Being thrown around,
The next minute,
I'm lying on the ground,
Being punched in the face
And in my side,
I try my best to run and hide!
I just keep *running!*
And when I stop . . . I come to find,
My money has gone!
Now I cannot eat!
But someday I will beat that . . .
                    that horrid bully!

Ryan Morrall (14)
Ysgol Bryn Elian, Colwyn Bay

A Dog's Life

A dog's life could be very fun,
Running around, sleeping
And playing all day long.

If I had a wish I'd wish I were a dog,
For being able to run and being so easily loved,
Getting loved is fun for a dog.

If I could run on all fours,
If I could understand what other dogs are saying,
If I could bark and talk to animals.

If only I had a wish,
If I could be a well-loved dog,
If I could be a big sheepdog.

I wish I could be a dog,
But I'm just a boy with high hopes,
I wish, I wish I was a dog.

Raeffe Roberts (12)
Ysgol Bryn Elian, Colwyn Bay

Family Problems

Today my sister and me are friends
It won't be long before our friendship ends
We hit and kick each other
Then along comes our brother
To split us up
Mum and Dad are throwing cups
Baby Laura is crying her eyes out
As I cry my heart out.

Madison Jones (14)
Ysgol Bryn Elian, Colwyn Bay

Gone

The feeling haunts me inside
The smile that makes me wonder
Where has he gone in this big world wide
No one to hold me through the thunder

Pictures hidden but not for long
For I can find them anywhere
Everything that has gone wrong
Now everything is there

My brother that look like him
Their eyes, their nose
For I could never win
The days that he owes

The day I wait
To know where I came from
What's the date?
But he is still gone.

Kirsty Palmer (14)
Ysgol Bryn Elian, Colwyn Bay

Snowflake

Down, down, down I fall,
Oh how I feel so small,
Twisting, turning, whirling and twirling,
Down, down, down I fall.

Faster and faster the water comes to me,
I think I'm about to hit the wavy sea,
Oh no, wait, here comes the wind,
Against an icy hull I am pinned.

Wait, oh wait, there is a final gust,
Out of the icy hull I am thrust,
Up into the sky, up so high,
Onto a bubbling sailor's pie.

James Clarke (13)
Ysgol Bryn Elian, Colwyn Bay

Walls

I am a wall
I'm covered in graffiti
My first name is Berlin
I used to live in Germany

My brother lives in China
And he is the longest
After all the years he has lasted
He's proved he is the strongest

My cousins live together
The four of them forever

My best mate Hadrian lives on a border
Been there since Roman times
You'll see him from space
Thank God he's doing fine.

Daniel Ashton (14)
Ysgol Bryn Elian, Colwyn Bay

Friends

Flowers may die
The sun may set
But you my friend I will never forget
Your name is engraved with letters of gold
It's the name that will never grow old

I've seen fire and rain
I've seen loneliness and pain
But I always thought I'd see you again.

Emma Howe (16)
Ysgol Bryn Elian, Colwyn Bay

Untitled

She sat beside her window
She gazed and looked around
The world losing its colours
She slowly felt a frown

She thought about her time here
She felt useless and small
Darkness began to fill her mind
Tears began to fall

In a world full of colours
She thought her life was fray
She sat on her own at night
Her light so dim and grey

She wished she was the other girls
Who laugh and sing and shout
But still she sits and wonders
What this pain is all about

She used to be happy
Saw colour in everything
But now she sits full of doubt
She's forgotten how to sing

One day she feels full of fear, that no one would care
If one day she disappeared

. . . One day she wasn't there.

Connor Ryan (14)
Ysgol Bryn Elian, Colwyn Bay

If I Were A King

If I were a king
I would rule all the land
And teach all the fish
To walk on the sand

Dogs would climb trees
And cats would stand guard
Ants would be teased
It wouldn't be hard

If I were a king
The wind wouldn't blow
And on Christmas Day
We would always have snow

There would be no school
Of that I am sure
The kids would be free
To run out the door

Oh well I guess being
A king is too hard
Right! Now I'm off
To play in the yard.

Daniel Davies (11)
Ysgol Bryn Elian, Colwyn Bay

Teenagers

We're not all bad
And may I add,
To assume is wrong,
This has gone on for too long,
Some of us feel victimised,
Which may make you surprised.

We're not all vandals
And we don't all like scandals,
Some of us are nice,
Which does not come at a price.

If a few friends go into a shop,
Even just to buy a bottle of pop,
The assistant is checking you're not going to steal,
It's so unfair, it's so unreal.

That's why I am writing in this book,
To tell you to just take a look,
Please don't judge every book by its cover,
Just look a little deeper and see what you might uncover.

Rachel Jones (14)
Ysgol Bryn Elian, Colwyn Bay

Teenagers

T roublemakers at times
E asily persuaded
E xaggerate little things
N ever on time
A lways late
G oing out
E very night
R eady for anything
S ometimes misunderstood.

Sam Edwards (15)
Ysgol Bryn Elian, Colwyn Bay

Football

It's that time of year again,
Men in shorts,
Pulling shirts,
Battling and tackling,
Kissing and cuddling,
Shooting and shouting,
Posing,
Pouting,
Penalty taking,
Muscles aching,
Injury faking,
The odd leg breaking.
By the end of the game,
Fans laying the blame - if they lost,
Directors counting the cost
Or jumping for joy if they won,
Celebrating victory goals.
For some it can be serious or fun,
For others
It's just football.

James Williams (14)
Ysgol Bryn Elian, Colwyn Bay

Shopaholic

S hopaholic Sian
H ours on end
O pening my purse
P aying with money
P arting with Mummy
I ndulging in KFCs
N ice for me
G oing now!

Sian Wilson (15)
Ysgol Bryn Elian, Colwyn Bay

I Am Love

If I could move a mountain,
I'd do it just for you,
Lift it into the sky,
That's what I'd do.

If I could paint a rainbow
And watch it with a smile,
I'd stay there with you,
Forever and a while.

If I could stop the moon
And be there with you all night,
We'd look up and watch,
To make our hearts alight.

If I could part the seas,
And be there yours and mine,
Holding your hand through all,
Extending through all the time.

If I could show how much I love you,
Time would even stand still,
To be here with you,
Forever, never, until . . .

Luke Woods (15)
Ysgol Bryn Elian, Colwyn Bay

I Love You

To tell you that I love you,
Means much more than words can say,
I can't describe the way I feel for you,
Each and every day.

But when I say I love you,
You know the words are true,
And this special little poem,
Brings all my love to you.

Lauren Giblin (15)
Ysgol Bryn Elian, Colwyn Bay

Fashion

Walking through the wardrobes,
A paradise of style,
The sound of Valentino,
Always makes me smile.

Surrounded by this stylish world,
The fantasy grows on,
Always the ecstatic thrill,
When wearing Louis Vuitton.

Leopard print and dogtooth,
All worn by Kate Moss,
Printed all over magazines,
It's all the latest goss.

This office filled with style,
It has been a long stint,
I am a top designer,
And my name is Ellie Flint!

Ellie Flint (14)
Ysgol Bryn Elian, Colwyn Bay

Girls And Boys

G orgeous and elegant
I diotic and extremely funny
R ebellious and nice
L iberated and free of thought
S oft on the inside, hard on the outside

A lways to be seen together
N ever seen to be alone
D otted about like decorations

B ullying all the time and having a laugh
O bnoxiously funny
Y elling like they are psycho
S ome things will never change; boys will be boys.

Leonie Mason (14)
Ysgol Bryn Elian, Colwyn Bay

My Mum

My mum is great,
She's my closest mate,
She's always there for me
And she's forever cooking tea!

Her food is delicious,
It's definitely not vicious.
It's not cold, it's not hot,
But it's frankly all I've got.

I love my mum
And she loves me too,
So whatever happens, Mum
I'm always there for you.

She's funny, she's a wally,
But she always keeps me jolly.

She's great, she's fine and she's
All *mine!*

Tamsin Davies (12)
Ysgol Bryn Elian, Colwyn Bay

Everton For Life

I proudly wear my blue shirt
And speak EFC with pride.
EFC is the greatest club,
It's something you just can't hide.

Andy Johnson goals galore,
Andy will score some more.
A goal machine for the Blues,
Watch this space, we cannot lose.

So give us a cheer at Goodison Park,
Even if the outcome is dark.
Everyone's drinking freezing cold coffees
And cheering on the mighty toffees.

Lewis Roberts (12)
Ysgol Bryn Elian, Colwyn Bay

Penguins

Far up north,
Where the cold winds blow,
The penguins come out,
To give a show.

It's always cold,
It's never hot,
What I'd give
For a delicious hot pot.

I hate the ice,
I hate my feet,
I hate blizzards
And I hate meat.

Goodbye for now
And go back to the heat,
Of your beautiful home
In a place called Crete.

Brad Carnell (13)
Ysgol Bryn Elian, Colwyn Bay

Stars!

I am a star way up high,
I look down on people passing by,
Watching lovers lie and stare,
Wondering what else hides up there.

Granting wishes, making dreams,
Magic powers, though it seems.
I am a star on a Christmas tree,
Seeing everyone smile at me.

Shooting stars they are your friends,
Make a wish, it will never end.
I am big, I am bold,
I shine over the whole world!

Paige Steward (13)
Ysgol Bryn Elian, Colwyn Bay

Ripper

Mist twists around her ankles
Her body shivers

The pitch-black London sky
Her only companion

Filled with self-hatred
It's for the family, for the family

Shadowy figure seeps through
The dark cold Whitechapel air

She adjusts her crimson bodice
A customer? She asks

He silently approaches
His face expressionless

His closed-mouth whispers
'I know a place where no one will pass'

The only sounds
Clicking of high heels and a hacking cough

Now hastily pushed against a wall
She hitches up her skirt

He laughs, his strong hands
Clasped firmly round her fragile throat

She chokes, stutters out her few last words
'Drain my blood, do your worst, I'm all yours baby.'

Becky Yarwood (14)
Ysgol Bryn Elian, Colwyn Bay

Stranded

As I trudge on through a shifting sea of sand,
The cruel sun beats down on me.
Every breath brings agony,
Every movement causes pain,
My skin is burnt red from sunburn,
My lips are cracked and blistered
And my legs are tired and weak
And vultures circle overhead.

But I trudge onward.

Suddenly my legs collapse underneath me
And I just lie there,
Too tired to get up
And I wonder,
What will happen now?

Abraham Carder (14)
Ysgol Bryn Elian, Colwyn Bay

Hostage

We are on an Easyjet plane,
The captors must be insane.
No one will dare to complain,
Or the captor may get out a cane!

They are asking for a pilot and fuel,
Otherwise it may result in a duel.
These people are really so cruel,
In this world they cannot rule!

On this plane we all feel frightened,
But then suddenly, this situation tightened.
A passenger became very enlightened,
As the situation brightened!

Sebastian Jones (14)
Ysgol Bryn Elian, Colwyn Bay

Handbag

Striding down the catwalk,
She stops to strike a pose,
I'm a Louis Vuitton original,
I'm made to match the clothes.

I started on the fashion channel
For every girl to see
Next to Gucci and Chanel
I'm lucky she picked me!

I'm a must have accessory
Belts, diamonds and shoes
For going out and partying
You can wear me with your Jimmy Choo's

I'm Victoria Beckham's favourite
Hear the shouts and screams
As she struts down the red carpet
I'm the handbag of your dreams!

Beth Jones (14)
Ysgol Bryn Elian, Colwyn Bay

Earth

Have been here for millions of years
I speak no words I cry no tears
Here you tread on my broken face
Battered and destroyed by the human race

Once full forest now lay bare
All cut down without a care
Ice caps melting, sea levels rising
I am dying without compromising

As I deteriorate day by day
Don't stand back my problem won't just go away
If everyone did just one simple thing
A lot more life to me it could bring.

Kirsty Morris (14)
Ysgol Bryn Elian, Colwyn Bay

The Racehorse

I was in the starting gate,
The gate came down
And I galloped down the straight,
I reached the first fence.

I was feeling very tense,
I soared through the air,
Landing safely on the ground,
I could hear the roar of the crowd.

Down the homeward stretch we go,
Faster, faster,
Through the wind we soar,
Now I hear them cheer for me!

I see the colours in the crowd,
See hopeful faces all around,
I hear the pounding hooves behind,
But the winning post is in my sight.

A final sprint
And I win the race,
A glorious ending,
A champion's right.

Katherine Edwards (14)
Ysgol Bryn Elian, Colwyn Bay

My Mates!

Abbie is a really ace mate,
There's nothing about her that I hate,
We've known each other all these years,
So all I have left to say is cheers.

Raxii Roo is her name,
Screaming and shouting is her game,
Without Raxii it wouldn't be right,
She's like a star that shines at night.

Holly's nickname is Holly Dolly,
She makes us all feel very jolly,
Everything she does is always fun,
When it's raining she brings out the sun.

George is small but very sweet,
But it doesn't matter about the size of her feet,
She's just like everyone else,
Singing, dancing and enjoying herself.

Tamsin is one of the mad ones in the bunch,
Especially during our hyper lunch,
She's not the cleverest person alive,
Although she can count to five.

Michelle's the quietest one of all,
She doesn't make much noise at all,
She sits with us all the time,
According to us that's just fine.

Well, well, well Alicia Wood,
I really don't know whether I should,
But she's my mate so I will,
All I can say is she's brill.

There you have it, all my friends,
I hope our friendship never ends.

Laura Rickard (13)
Ysgol Bryn Elian, Colwyn Bay

The Boarding School

The wall is grey,
The ceiling's green,
I'm really bored
And the teacher's mean.

There're holes in the floor,
There are no chairs,
We stand up all day
And cut open hares.

Monday is havoc,
Tuesday is hell,
Don't think about Wednesday,
It kicks up a smell.

Thursday is wet,
Friday is dry,
The ground's like a bog
And the groundskeeper cries.

Cockroach for breakfast,
Gerbils for tea,
The dinner lady's coming,
So it's now time to flee.

The Head is too evil,
The Deputy's too thick,
Maths teacher's too useless
And they all need a kick.

The wall is grey,
The ceiling's green,
I'm really bored
And the teacher's mean.

Thomas Eckett (14)
Ysgol Bryn Elian, Colwyn Bay

Jade Goody

Through the cheering crowd
It started off so well
I enjoyed it while it lasted
Now my life is hell

Another TV show
My career down the drain
Everything I have
Is all from my fame

People think I'm a racist
And everyone hates me
My life is now in pieces
And it's all because of me

Everything I worked for
Slowly drifts away
All the pain and hurt
Forever it will stay.

Natasha Moyler (14)
Ysgol Bryn Elian, Colwyn Bay

My Parents

There are these people,
They are special to me,
They come in groups of two,
Not in groups of three.

One of them is big, one very small,
My dad is the one who is very tall.

My mum is as small as can be,
She cooks tea for my dad and me.
My dad is muscly, he goes weight training,
But when he was in school he got a good caning,

So there they are,
As good as can be,
The people who are always there for me.

Georgina Roberts (12)
Ysgol Bryn Elian, Colwyn Bay

I Had Someone Special

I had someone special,
That was so dear to me,
All the memories we shared,
Picnics under the tree,
He was kind,
He was gentle,
He would take care of me,
He would tell me his stories,
While sipping his tea,
He became very ill
And I thought he'd pull through,
Day in and day out he lay very still,
I had someone special
And then he was gone,
I went to the church
To sing him a song,
I once had a grandad,
I still have him now,
I will miss him forever,
So farewell to thou.

Tessa Jones (13)
Ysgol Bryn Elian, Colwyn Bay

Teenagers

T roublemakers
E gging houses
E veryone the same
N agging parents
A rguing with siblings
G etting in trouble
E xtremely annoying
R ejecting all the rules
S tereotyping really hurts

Teenagers are really not that bad.

Becky Jones (12)
Ysgol Bryn Elian, Colwyn Bay

I Am A Spider

I am a spider
I am scary
I have eight legs
And they're all hairy

I live on a web
I also eat flies
I swing on my silk
And roll my eight eyes

At people I frighten
At people I scare
They squash me with the paper
No one seems to care

I am a spider
I am scary
If you look through my eight eyes
Humans are really scary.

Berwyn Roberts (14)
Ysgol Bryn Elian, Colwyn Bay

Sunset Bay

I'm galloping on the beach
With the wind in my mane
With my rider holding my reins
'Faster,' she shouts, 'wee hee!'
After the ride we glide home together
We will stay with each other
Forever and ever.

Hollie Louise Griffith (12)
Ysgol Bryn Elian, Colwyn Bay

My Dad

There is a man
And it's my dad
I was his little princess
A life it used to be

One day he went
Just drove away
The pain it made me feel
You couldn't imagine it, it's unreal

Tears sliding down my face
Not a goodbye to be heard
Or a hug to feel
I wish it were a nightmare

But it has to be real
Doesn't it?

Raquel Evans (13)
Ysgol Bryn Elian, Colwyn Bay

Black And White Cat

One black and white cat,
Cleaning his fur.
You can stroke him
And he'll start to purr.
Sometimes he's bad,
Sometimes he's good,
Put dinner on the table and he'd snatch it if he could.
Once he climbed up a broken ladder,
Got past my dad as he was watching Blackadder.
He reached the top and then he fell,
Then we had to ring the neighbour's bell.
Few days later he was back on his feet,
Chasing mice on the cold concrete.
So there's our cat, our black and white cat,
Who's sleeping next to his favourite toy rat.

Daniel Hardwick (14)
Ysgol Bryn Elian, Colwyn Bay

Pet Shop Journey!

I can't believe it's happening,
My dad has made the date,
I've been waiting for two weeks,
To get my brand new mate.

We are on our way now,
To get another pet
And Dad's already moaning
About the costs at the vet.

I see a furry animal,
It's a huge black rat,
But it's screeching and it's scratching,
I couldn't cope with that!

A fluffy white rabbit,
Hopping in the straw,
I've got enough hairy animals
And I don't want any more.

We walk around the shop again
And see a big blue bird,
But the twittering it's making,
I find that noise absurd.

A scary hairy spider,
Looking me in the eye,
If I saw that at night,
I would very nearly die.

Then I see a little creature,
He's green and makes no noise
And now I have decided on
My very own tortoise.

Alicia Wood (13)
Ysgol Bryn Elian, Colwyn Bay

Fire-Breathing Dragon

I'm a fire-breathing dragon,
Who likes to go out at night.
I like to eat tin food,
I'm talking about a knight.

If anybody sees me,
I'll have to get away
And if another dragon comes,
It just might become my prey.

I'll be scared of course,
But never mind,
I might just win
With my hands tied.

And that's the story
Of my whole life,
The fire-breathing dragon,
Back to my life of strife.

Samuel Williams (12)
Ysgol Bryn Elian, Colwyn Bay

Bullying

I feel very upset when people leave me out,
I just want to give them a clout.

I'm on my own in the playground
And then I find a cat in a mound.

The cat was lonely just like me,
Rolled up in a ball and crying.

The cat was so weak,
It was close to dying.

Then I realised we were the same,
Both caught up in the same stupid game.

I feel very happy now,
I've got a friend but how?

Steph Dennis (13)
Ysgol Bryn Elian, Colwyn Bay

You'll Never Walk Alone

In the morning get out of bed
Feed the kids
Now they're fed

Go to training, shoot one-two
Show the team
What you can do

Go to the game, get some fame
2-1 up
We're still in the cup

A header he made
In the back of the net it stayed
United are out without a doubt

Liverpool are through
They are so true
You'll never walk alone.

Joshua Birtles (13)
Ysgol Bryn Elian, Colwyn Bay

Baby In A Cot!

I'm newborn today,
I'm helpless in my small cot,
Giants by my bed.

Big hands touching me,
I'm scared of the giants here now,
Come Mother quickly.

I wail and burble,
'They are not here to hurt you,'
Mother comforts me.

Bottle is ready,
My milk flowing down my throat,
Off I go to sleep.

I'm safe now!

Billie May Blundell (12)
Ysgol Bryn Elian, Colwyn Bay

Driven To Insanity!

Poke me!
Prod me!
Lock me in a chokey!
But you *won't* get it out of me, no you *won't!*

Torch me!
Scorch me!
Throw me in a cage!
But you *can't* get it out of me, no you *can't!*

Stab me!
Grab me!
Chuck me on a taxi!
But you *shan't* get it out of me, no you *shan't!*

OK!
You . . . poked me, you prodded me, you locked me in a chokey!
You . . . torched me, you scorched me, you threw me in a cage!
You . . . stabbed me, you grabbed me then chucked me on a taxi!
So I confess!

After you . . . you . . . poked me, then prodded me, you locked me
                                                        in a chokey!
You . . . torched me, then scorched me, you threw me in a cage!
You stabbed me, then grabbed me and chucked me on a taxi!
And my confession is now, you've driven me to *insanity!*

Charlotte Burgess (12)
Ysgol Bryn Elian, Colwyn Bay

Hungry Africans

African children are ill
And on their bill

With no family to love them
They have no home

Working so young
With nothing on their feet

Some shoes would be nice
So would something to eat

They live in tents like little ants
Beast and child living in the wild

Disease is awful, killing their families
Next it might be you

No one really cares
And the world just stares

It seems so unfair
But . . .

Tomos Williams (12)
Ysgol Bryn Elian, Colwyn Bay

Myself

Eyes green as grass
And white like clouds,
My eyes.

At writing, dumb as a sheep,
At playing, clever as a fox.

Tall as a house,
Friendly as a mouse.

Nobody's like me,
That's me,
Myself.

Robin Owen (11)
Ysgol Dyffryn Nantlle, Caernarfon

Alone

Darkness begins to swallow me up,
Tears pour like blood from a deep wound,
The clock strikes midnight,
It seems to have been forever,
Since yesterday.

I feel sick with fear,
Sad and lonely,
An empty longing,
But for what?

I'm isolated,
In this life,
I want to blast my head open,
The pain is too much.

The darkness has swallowed me up,
Utterly, completely,
Forever,
Alone.

Llinos Ann Williams (13)
Ysgol Gyfyn Llangefni, Llangefni